Withdrawn

CULTURES OF THE WORLD
Spain

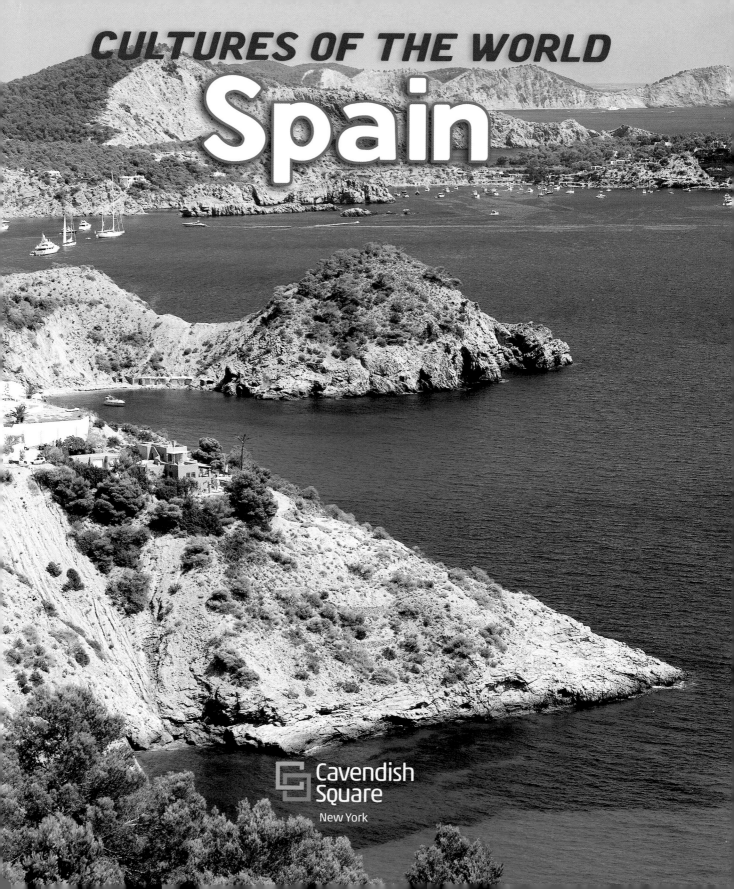

Cavendish Square

New York

Published in 2014 by Cavendish Square Publishing, LLC
303 Park Avenue South, Suite 1247, New York, NY 10010

Third Edition

This publication is published with arrangement with Marshall Cavendish International (Asia) Pte Ltd.

Copyright © 2014 Marshall Cavendish International (Asia) Pte Ltd.

Website: cavendishsq.com

Cultures of the World is a registered trademark of Times Publishing Limited.

This publication represents the opinions and views of the author based on his or her personal experience, knowledge, and research. The information in this book serves as a general guide only. The author and publisher have used their best efforts in preparing this book and disclaim liability rising directly or indirectly from the use and application of this book.

CPSIA Compliance Information: Batch #WS13CSQ

All websites were available and accurate when this book was sent to press.

Library of Congress Cataloging-in-Publication Data
Kohen, Elizabeth, 1960-
 Spain / Elizabeth Kohen, Marie Louise Elias, Josie Elias. — 3rd ed.
   p. cm. — (Cultures of the world)
 Includes bibliographical references and index.
 Summary: "Provides comprehensive information on the geography, history, wildlife, governmental structure, economy, cultural diversity, peoples, religion, and culture of Spain"—Provided by publisher.
 ISBN 978-1-60870-871-0 (hardcover) ISBN 978-1-62712-162-0 (paperback) ISBN 978-1-60870-877-2 (ebook)
 1. Spain—Juvenile literature. I. Elias, Marie Louise. II. Elias, Josie. III. Title.

 DP17.K6 2013
 946—dc23   2012017640

Writers: Elizabeth Kohen, Marie Louise Elias, Josie Elias
Editors: Deborah Grahame-Smith, Mindy Pang
Copyreader: Tara Tomczyk
Designers: Nancy Sabato, Benson Tan
Cover picture researcher: Tracey Engel
Picture researcher: Joshua Ang

PICTURE CREDITS
Cover: © Hemis.fr / SuperStock
Audrius Tomonis - www.banknotes.com: 135 • Corbis / Click Photos: 32, 59, 101 • Getty Images: 5, 22, 38, 40, 41, 50, 71, 99, 123 • Inmagine.com: 1, 3, 6, 9, 10, 11, 12, 13, 14, 15, 16, 17, 18, 20, 21, 23, 25, 26, 28, 29, 30, 33, 36, 39, 42, 43, 44, 46, 47, 48, 49, 51, 52, 53, 54, 55, 56, 57, 58, 60, 61, 62, 63, 64, 65, 66, 67, 68, 69, 72, 73, 74, 75, 76, 77, 79, 81, 84, 85, 86, 87, 88, 92, 93, 94, 95, 97, 100, 102, 104, 105, 106, 107, 109, 110, 113, 114, 116, 117, 118, 120, 125, 127, 128, 130, 131 • Northwind Picture Archives: 24 • Marshall Cavendish Archives: 35 • Topfoto: 27 • Wikimedia commons: 96

PRECEDING PAGE
An island on the Mediterranean Sea, Ibiza is the third-largest of the Balearic Islands archipelago.

Printed in the United States of America

CONTENTS

SPAIN TODAY

AT THE CULTURAL CROSSROADS OF EUROPEAN AND MOORISH influences, Spain is rich in beauty and contrasts. From rugged mountain ranges to soft-sand beaches, from dazzling white cities to Gothic cathedrals and mosques, from colorful religious festivals to dramatic bullfights, Spain beguiles the senses.

One of the most ancient countries in Europe, Spain has survived numerous conquerors and conquests, religious fervor, and expansionism. It has seen power and glory during the days of the Catholic kings, and then watched it all decline as days of darkness and obscurity later followed: unstable rule, civil war, and right-wing fanaticism. Today, however, Spain is enjoying renewed cultural splendor. With the introduction of new and controversial austerity measures, it is hoped that progress is being made toward creating a stable economy.

Renowned for its sunshine and beaches, Spain also has a rich culture of traditions and festivals. Spain boasts a fascinating history and many famous historic sites that are unique and inspirational. There are quaint and charming villages that time seems to have passed by, as well as modern vibrant cities such as Madrid and Barcelona.

Famous for having Christian, Jewish, and Muslim influences, Toledo was declared a World Heritage Site by UNESCO in 1986 for being one of the former capitals of the Spanish empire.

Nature reserves with beautiful and dramatic scenery are home to many of the Iberian Peninsula's unique flora and fauna.

Spanish people are very proud of their history and culture and are usually delighted if foreigners take an interest. The Spanish way of life is somewhat slower than in the rest of Europe, particularly in the south. Some cultures believe the tradition of a rest in the afternoon, the siesta, is lazy, but when the Spanish work, they work hard. In 2006 employees of the central government adopted a new schedule, eliminating the long midday break. The one-hour lunch break was introduced in order to align the Spanish work schedule with the rest of Europe's, and to reduce the length of time that workers, particularly working parents, spend away from home. Spanish employees work, on average, 38.5 hours per the standard five days a week from Monday to Friday, whereas the weekly European average is only 36.8 hours per week.

Public holidays fall on the same date each year but can vary slightly depending on whether the day of celebration or feast day falls on a Sunday. There are many regional holidays as some areas have their own feast days to commemorate certain patron saints. On the national holidays, all banks will definitely be closed but some businesses may choose to stay open, as do some stores. If the national holiday is on a Tuesday or a Thursday, many Spaniards will also take the week's Monday or Friday as a holiday. This is called a *puente* and means "to make a bridge" so that they get a four-day weekend. This is not, and never has been, official policy. But it is common practice and widely accepted. To increase productivity Prime Minister Mariano Rajoy announced in 2012 that most holidays that fall mid-week will be moved to a Monday or a Friday. This will limit workers to a three-day weekend.

There are 42 properties in Spain inscribed on the UNESCO World Heritage list, including the Old Towns of Ávila, Cáceres, Córdoba, Cuenca, Santiago de Compostela, Segovia, Tarragona, and Toledo. Also on the list are the Alhambra, Generalife, and Albayzín, in Granada; the Cathedral, Alcázar, and Archivo de Indias in Seville; the Roman archaeological sites of Mérida and Tárraco; the Roman walls of Lugo; the prehistoric rock art sites in the Coa Valley and Siega Verde; the Royal Monastery of Santa Maria de Guadalupe; and the Caves of Altamira. There are also three parks that have been designated as World Heritage sites: Doñana National Park, Garajonay National Park, and Teide National Park. The island of Ibiza is on the UNESCO World Heritage List for Biodiversity and Culture. Madrid and Barcelona are both popular cities for a weekend break as they are both historically significant, have some superb architecture, and have an excellent choice of stores. Vacationers with young families tend to go to the beautiful coastal areas, such as the Costa Blanca, Costa Brava, and Costa del Sol.

Spanish people enjoy their free time with a walk in the park, a swim at the beach, or meeting their friends in a café. There are many clubs for Spaniards as well as foreigners, which cater to enthusiasts of many different hobbies and leisure pursuits from stamp collecting to paragliding. Popular family-oriented outdoor leisure time activities in Spain include walking, fishing, golf, football, and tennis. A vibrant cultural life, with events that span the arts and suit a whole range of audiences, is popular with Spaniards and also makes Spain a magnet for visitors from around the world. Art and music take the lead but dance, theater, architecture, literature, and media arts are also important. Live music is very popular and in many towns and cities the evenings and nights buzz with sounds of music from around the world.

Spain has a population of roughly 47 million people. Approximately 12 percent of the Spanish population is made up of foreign nationals, comprising about 861,000 Romanians, 777,000 Moroccans, 380,000 Ecuadorians, 200,000 Colombians, and 180,000 Italians, besides the 226,000 British people registered as residents in Spain, and an estimated one million Britons who spend at least a part of the year in this country. But after a decade of high immigration and rapid population growth, Spain's population is now declining. The current economic and financial crisis has thrown the population growth into reverse, with thousands of people, both foreigners and young Spaniards, leaving the country because they have been unable to find work.

At the beginning of 2012 Spain's inflation rate rose to 3 percent and the unemployment rate to 23 percent, which equates to approximately 5 million people unemployed. The highest number of job losses has been in service industries and the construction industry. Spain is facing the risk of another recession, and the debt crisis makes it questionable whether the Popular Party center-right government can deliver the swift turnaround that financial markets are demanding.

Spain has embarked on a major program of fiscal adjustment, spending cuts, and tax increases. Value added tax (VAT) is an excise tax based on the value added to certain products at each stage of production or distribution. VAT has recently been increased by 2 percent and there have been big cuts in civil service pay and in other sectors, such as public education and health. Gross domestic product (GDP) represents the total monetary value of all services and goods produced over a specified time period. In an effort to close a budget deficit expected to reach 8 percent of GDP, Prime Minister Rajoy announced an austerity package made up of $16.15 billion by way of tax increases and $36 billion in spending cuts, which resulted in civil unrest and demonstrations in major cities. In February 2012 student protests in the city of Valencia against budget cuts ended in clashes with the police, several injuries, and the arrest of 25 protesters. The next day thousands of people demonstrated after accusing the police of using violence during the previous day's protest. Prime Minister Rajoy appealed for calm, but the general mood in Spain remains unsettled.

Mariano Rajoy's conservative People's Party won a landslide victory in Spain's general election of November 2012. Because of this outright majority the government has not had to make a pact with any opposition party. The government is trying to stimulate the economy by changing employment laws, but trade unions say that workers' rights are being eroded. Changes approved by Mariano Rajoy's conservative government to reduce severance pay and give employers greater flexibility over jobs has led to mass rallies in Madrid, Barcelona, Valencia, and Seville against the conservative government's labor market reforms. The labor law reforms are designed to encourage companies and businesses to hire more people by offering tax breaks for taking on young people and by cutting government-mandated severance packages. The youth unemployment rate is approaching 50 percent—that is, one out of every two youths between the age of 16 and 24 is unemployed even though some of those youngsters have one, and sometimes two, university degrees. Young Spaniards are now living in the family home for even longer than before, in some cases not becoming independent from their parents until they are into their thirties. In America just over 18 percent of young adults under the age of 25 are unemployed.

Spanish society is considering the changes that will have to take place in various areas within the coming decades in order to achieve a balance among the productive sectors. Apart from the austerity measures introduced by the government, there are four main courses of action to be implemented. Energy savings and efficiency are to be increased, reducing the consumption of fossil fuels by harnessing renewable energy sources such as wind and water power. The development of these alternative and renewable sources of energy will not only be a means to reducing energy dependence but will also become a competitive industry. New technologies and innovations are to be promoted in every production process to make them more cost-effective and efficient. New information technologies are to be introduced and expanded so that the number of households with broadband Internet access is increased.

Wind turbines on an agricultural field in Castile, Spain.

Spain has a largely urban population and it is intended to make modifications within the towns and cities to improve the quality of life. Efforts to improve air quality will be pursued, streets will be pedestrianized, and energy will be used more efficiently. Metropolitan areas will streamline the use of transport by improving the suburban train services and the urban bus and tram lines.

There is no doubt that Spain is currently experiencing a very challenging period, with a recession looming, high unemployment, demonstrations over government cuts and labor law reforms, increased taxes, high inflation, and an increasing crime rate. It is to be hoped that the austerity measures introduced by the Mariano Rajoy government in 2012 will be enough to divert the crisis and allow Spain to get back on track for a successful and prosperous economic future.

GEOGRAPHY

The evening light brings out a spritely palette of colors on this beach in Fuerteventura, the second-largest island of the Canary Islands.

1

S PAIN, EUROPE'S third-largest nation, is more than twice the size of the state of Oregon. It occupies most of the Iberian Peninsula at the western edge of the continent and has an area of 195,124 square miles (505,370 square kilometers), including the Balearic and Canary islands.

The Spanish territory includes the mainland (about 98 percent of the national territory), the Balearic Islands in the Mediterranean Sea, the Canary Islands off the western coast of Africa, the Spanish free ports of Ceuta and Melilla on the northern coast of Africa in Morocco, and several other small islands off the coast of Morocco.

An aerial view of the rural landscape near Castile-La Mancha in Toledo.

Spain occupies 85 percent of the Iberian Peninsula, which it shares with Portugal, in southwest Europe. It is bounded on the north by the Bay of Biscay, France, and Andorra, on the east by the Mediterranean Sea, on the south by the Atlantic Ocean and the Mediterranean Sea, and on the west by Portugal and the Atlantic Ocean. The 8-mile-wide (13-km-wide) Strait of Gibraltar separates Spain from Africa in the southwest.

The Praia das Catedrais, or "Beach of the Cathedrals," in Galicia is characterized by green moss and natural rock formations.

Spain borders France and Andorra in the north and Portugal in the west. The eastern and southern coasts of Spain border the Mediterranean Sea. One of Spain's most striking geographical features is the extensive range of mountains found in the north and south of the country and on the offshore islands. The second-highest country in Europe, after Switzerland, Spain has an average elevation of 2,165 feet (660 meters); a quarter of its surface area rises above 3,000 feet (985 m).

Another remarkable feature is the Meseta, a plateau in the center of the country. Making up almost half of the Spanish mainland, it is the largest plateau of its kind in Europe, extending over 81,000 square miles (210,000 square km) with an average elevation of 2,165 feet (660 m). Spain also boasts a coastline some 3,084 miles (4,964 km) long. This highly varied topography makes for an interesting diversity in both climate and natural resources.

MAINLAND REGIONS

The Spanish mainland can be broadly divided into five distinct regions:

GREEN SPAIN Located in the north and northwest, Green Spain includes the regions of Galicia, Asturias, Cantabria, and the Basque provinces. Green Spain has a wet, evergreen climate typical of more northwestern European countries such as England. Moss-covered rock formations and ancient ruins lie scattered in this mostly rural landscape. The coastline is rugged, especially in the west, with steep cliffs and great rocky inlets called *rías* (REE-uhs).

The Cantabrian Mountains, which extend roughly 180 miles (289 km) through north and northwestern Spain and rise to 8,688 feet (2,648 m) at

their highest point, form a natural barrier between Green Spain and the rest of the country and feature some of the country's wildest landscapes. The Basque countryside to the northeast features an unusual mix of idyllic mountain villages and a concentration of engineering industries, shipbuilding facilities, and chemical plants.

INLAND SPAIN Consisting of the provinces of La Rioja, Castile-León, Castile—La Mancha, Extremadura, and the capital Madrid, this region is characterized by its elevated plateaus and arid climate. The province of Madrid has a population of 5.9 million, and the city of Madrid, with a population of 2.9 million, has been Spain's capital since the 16th century.

Surrounding Madrid province is a distinctive scenery and terrain. The Sierra de Guadarrama and Sierra de Gredos to the north and west of Madrid provide perfect winter playgrounds, while the land to the south of Madrid is harsh and sun-baked. La Rioja, a small region of farmland northeast of Madrid, is known for its extensive vineyards. The huge region of Castile surrounding Madrid includes the ancient kingdoms of Castile and León as well as the region of La Mancha.

Cabretón in La Rioja boasts beautiful tracts of agricultural land and a rolling, hilly landscape.

The Pyrenees mountains in Andorra. Andorra is a principality between France and Spain that is ruled by both countries.

The entire region is located on a vast plateau, the Meseta, which has a melancholic appearance. A stony landscape is a dominant feature of the Castilian countryside; the fields surrounding the cities of Ávila and Segovia are littered with boulders. The soil is poor here, as it also is in Extremadura, a wild remote region that has not been transformed by modernization and thus provides a glimpse into an older Spain.

THE PYRENEES This rugged mountain chain extends 270 miles (434 km) along the Spanish-French border from the Bay of Biscay to the Gulf of Valencia and rises to 11,169 feet (3,404 m) at Pico de Aneto, the highest point. The Pyrenees includes three main ranges: the Catalan Pyrenees, the central Pyrenees in Aragón, and the Pyrenees of Navarre. The regions of Navarre and Aragón, both former medieval kingdoms, abut the Pyrenees.

Throughout this mountainous region, there are upper meadows, pastureland, glacial lakes, and streams. At the foot of the mountains lies a series of valleys that turn to fertile orchards and vineyards at the Ebro River basin.

MEDITERRANEAN SPAIN This area includes the regions of Catalonia, Valencia, and Murcia. The region of Catalonia is geographically the most diverse. In the shadow of the northeastern portion of the Pyrenees, Catalonia's landscape changes from cold valleys to fertile *huertas* (wehr-tahs), coastal or irrigated plains rich with citrus orchards. Barcelona, the capital of Catalonia, has a population of about 2.1 million.

Valencia, too, is home to many citrus orchards and palm and fig trees. Murcia is the smallest and driest part of the Mediterranean region. Its irrigated hillsides, dotted with fertile *huertas*, are widely known for yielding excellent produce.

SOUTHERN SPAIN With a mild climate all year-round in most of the region, Andalusia is one of the top tourist spots in Spain. Nowhere else is the legacy of 750 years of Moorish occupation so evident. The Moorish fortress and palace complex of the Alhambra was the seat of government for ruling Moors until they were exiled in 1491.

The natural landscape of this region varies from east to west. In the east lie the majestic snow-capped mountains of the Sierra Nevada, whose peak Mulhacén is the highest point on the mainland, rising to 11,421 feet (3,481 m). High on these slopes are numerous little mountain villages. The fertile plains of Granada, lying at the foot of the Sierra Nevada, brim with tobacco fields and poplar groves. The dry desert landscape of the coastal city of Almería contrasts with the fertile soils and plains of cities only miles away.

The Mediterranean coast of Costa Blanca in Valencia. Especially beautiful is the Old Town of Altea due to the views from the town's main square and the bright Mediterranean light.

The Guadalquivir, known to the Arabs as the Wadi Al-Kabir, this "Great River" courses 408 miles (657 km) west through Andalusia to the Atlantic Ocean. The river crosses the olive groves of Jaén and the fruit and nut orchards of Córdoba. The fertile flat pastures, vineyards, and mostly white sand beaches of western Andalusia contrast with the mountain provinces in the east.

The banks of the Guadalquivir are lined with cotton and rice fields, citrus groves, and ranches that breed *toros bravos* (TOH-rohs BRAH-bos), bulls for the bullring.

Seville is the capital of Andalusia and the third-largest city in Spain, with a population of about 685,000. According to an ancient legend, Seville was actually founded by Hercules while he was on his adventures. The ancient city known to the Romans as Gades, modern-day Cádiz, is also in Andalusia. Located on the Atlantic coast Cádiz was founded by the Phoenicians around 1100 B.C. and proudly claims to be the oldest continuously inhabited city in the Western world.

Designed by the architect Jürgen Mayer-Hermann and completed in 2011, the iconic Metropol Parasol wooden building in the old quarter of Seville offers one of the best views of the city center.

THE CANARY AND BALEARIC ISLANDS

The Canary Islands are an archipelago of seven islands in the Atlantic Ocean, near the Tropic of Cancer and opposite the African coast. The nearest island is 67 miles (107 km) off the northwest African mainland. The islands are of volcanic origin, with varied geological formations and abundant tropical vegetation. There are also desert-like areas rich in minerals, black lava cliffs, and rare botanical species. The climate is warm and dry all year-round. On the island of Tenerife, Pico de Teide, the highest point in all of Spain, rises to 12,198 feet (3718 m).

The Balearic Islands lie 50 to 190 miles (80 to 305 km) from eastern Spain's Mediterranean coast, a position that made the islands an important

The islands and clear, turquoise-blue waters of Es Vedra Cala d'Hort in Ibiza.

strategic post for invaders and settlers throughout Spain's history. There are three main islands—Majorca, Minorca, and Ibiza—each with a distinctive character. Majorca, mountainous in the northwest, hilly in the southeast, and flat and full of olive and almond groves elsewhere, is the largest island of the group (five times the size of either Minorca or Ibiza) and the site of Palma, the Balearic capital. Ibiza is world-renowned as a popular vacation spot. Megalithic monuments from pre-Roman cultures are found on Minorca and Majorca.

CLIMATE

Spain's climate is generally less temperate than that in the rest of Europe, except in the north and northwest of the country where mild and wet conditions prevail with 31 to 59 inches (80 to 150 centimeters) of rain a year and temperatures of around 48°F (9°C) in winter and 64°F (18°C) in summer.

Summers in inland Spain are hot, with sporadic rainfall (as little as 15 inches, or 40 cm, per year), while winters are cold. Temperatures of 5°F (-15°C) in winter are common in the interior, and summer temperatures normally reach 80°F (27°C). Along the Mediterranean coast and in Andalusia and the Balearic Islands, a summer drought can at times last up to five months, even resulting in an annual rainfall of less than 24 inches (61 cm). Winter temperatures here hover around 52°F (11°C). In the summer, though, they rise to 95°F (35°C). Snowfall in Spain is infrequent except in the mountains.

FLORA AND FAUNA

Spain's regional differences in geography and climate provide a rich variety of vegetation and animal life.

GREEN SPAIN AND THE PYRENEES

Dense forests and grazing land form the perfect environment for mountain fauna such as ibex (wild goats), jabalí (wild boar), chamois, rabbits, and birds like partridge and quail. The European wolf (*Canis lupus*) and a species of wild brown bear (*Ursus arctos*) also live here. Brown bears are endangered in the Pyrenees due to loss of habitat and hunting, even though they are a protected species. In 1996 the French government released two pregnant female brown bears in the Pyrenees, followed by a single male a year later. These bears were brought from Slovenia, a natural habitat of the brown bear. The three bears, and their five offspring born in the wild, have spent long periods in forests of the Vall d'Aran, Pallars, and the Alta Ribagorça on the Spanish side of the mountains. Today a female, male, and at least four of the cubs survive.

The trees in these regions are primarily beech, oak, chestnut, and eucalyptus, and some pine and fir. Apple orchards can be found along the base of mountain ranges in areas such as Asturias, and half-wild horses, the Galician pony, roam the meadows of Galicia. The north coast of Spain is also known for its abundance of seafood. Scallops, hake, salmon, and trout populate the nearby rivers and seas.

THE MEDITERRANEAN COAST   Seafood and shellfish are abundant here. Rice fields dot Valencia's outskirts. Vineyards, olive groves, palm trees, and almond, fig, and citrus orchards are characteristic of the Mediterranean landscape.

ANDALUSIA The flora and fauna are typical of a subtropical climate. Olive groves, vineyards, and orchards of cherry, pear, peach, apricot, and almond

Almond trees in blossom. Spain also produces citrus fruit, grapes, apples, pears, apricots, figs, peaches, and many other kinds of fruits.

trees are common in the East. In the West, cotton, rice, and oranges are the predominant crops, and bulls are bred for the bullring. On the estuary of the Guadalquivir River lies Doñana National Park, one of the most important European refuges for wild animals. Endangered wildlife such as the Iberian lynx (*Lynx pardinus*) and the Spanish imperial eagle (*Acquila adalberti*) find shelter here.

THE CANARY ISLANDS   The volcanic soil and African coastal climate produce interesting vegetation. The dragon tree (*Dracaena draco*), native to these islands, was once thought to be the source of dragon's blood, because the orange fruit of the tree contains a thick, red, inedible liquid. Even today the tree seems mysterious, with its thick trunk and clusters of huge sword-shaped leaves. On the island of Tenerife, the oldest and tallest dragon tree reaches a height of 55 feet (17 m) and has a diameter of 66 feet (20 m) at the base. Extensive plantations of coffee, papayas, and bananas are also common throughout the islands.

A rare species of oleander grows in the center of the island of La Gomera. This variety of the green shrub, with its fragrant white or purple flowers, is considered a "living fossil," a remnant of a past geological age.

INTERNET LINKS

www.iberianature.com/

This is an English-language online source of information on the weather, geography, and history of Spain.

http://populations.guide-spain.com/

This website contains detailed population statistics for Spain.

http://whc.unesco.org/en/list/685

This website provides information, an interactive map, and photo gallery relating to the Doñana National Park in Andalusia.

HISTORY

Historians and tourists alike are drawn to the remains of ancient megalithic stone structures found at Menorca.

2

SPAIN'S UNIQUE LOCATION ON THE Iberian Peninsula has helped to create a history distinct from much of the rest of Europe. Mountain ranges and bodies of water separating Spain from the rest of the continent isolated the country from popular European culture and trends.

On the other hand, Spain's proximity to Africa led to invasions that brought rich cultural influences. Proximity to the Atlantic Ocean in turn gave Spain access to new territories in the Americas.

Built of unmortared, brick-like granite blocks in the first century A.D., Segovia's Roman aqueduct still supplies water to the city.

The Iberian Peninsula has been populated since prehistoric times. Modern humans made their appearance around 35,000 B.C. Around 4000 B.C. much of Spain was inhabited by the Iberians, arriving from the East. The Celts arrived later, followed by the Phoenicians around 1100 B.C. The Romans took the helm for six centuries, laying the foundations for Spanish language and culture.

EARLY SPAIN

Evidence suggests that Spain has been inhabited for nearly a million years. The caves of the Sierra de Atapuerca, in the northeastern corner of Castilian plateau, contain a fossil record of the earliest human beings in Europe. Bones and tools of early humans have also been found at other Spanish sites. The most impressive Stone Age remains are the polychrome paintings of bison, horses, and other animals on the ceilings of the caves at Altamira from some 15,000 years ago, in the Upper Paleolithic.

Evidence of Copper Age cultures has been found in southern Spain, as well as large stone tombs known as dolmens that were created by the Iberian people and date back 5,000 years.

From 1100 B.C. the earliest waves of immigrants brought in new cultural influences. From northern Africa came the Phoenicians, who colonized Cádiz and Almuñécar, and the Greeks, who made their settlements in Málaga and Ampurias. Some Phoenician and Greek inscriptions from this period still exist today. From the north came the Celts, an Indo-European people who settled in the northwest of Spain and later had considerable influence in northern Spain. In 225 B.C. Carthaginians founded Cartagena and Barcelona, eventually spreading over much of the Iberian Peninsula.

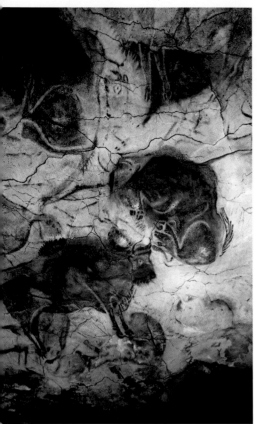

Cave paintings at Altamira, in northern Spain, are among the most remarkable prehistoric paintings ever discovered.

THE ROMAN CONQUEST

Rome invaded Iberia in 206 B.C. and expelled the Carthaginians. Over the next 200 years the Romans conquered the entire peninsula. Spain proved to be a valuable colony for Rome; indigenous metals such as gold, silver, copper, iron, tin, and lead enriched the empire.

However, Rome's influence on Spain was more permanent. The language, religion, and law of Spain today all stem from the Roman period, and many structures built by Roman engineers are still standing, including the aqueduct of Segovia, the theater at Mérida, and the bridge of Córdoba.

VISIGOTHIC SPAIN

Early in the fifth century Iberia was invaded by Germanic tribes. Among those who settled in Spain were the Vandals, who gave their name to Andalusia, and the Visigoths, who had the most influence and soon subdued the Vandals. The Visigoths established a kingdom in the northern regions and made Toledo their capital; by the seventh century, the last of the Roman strongholds along the southern coast fell to them. However, the Visigothic monarchy was not strong enough to withstand an invasion in A.D. 711 by a Muslim army from North Africa, which swept into Andalusia and destroyed the Christian Visigothic kingdom.

MUSLIM SPAIN

By A.D. 718 the Moors, as the Muslims were called by the Christians, controlled almost the entire Iberian Peninsula. Many Christians converted to Islam, and more Muslims of many nationalities—Arabs, Syrians, and Amazigh—settled in southern Spain, whose rich lands were more attractive than the deserts of North Africa. The Moors renamed Andalusia, which the Vandals had called Vandalusia, al-Andalus. The barren highlands of Castile in central Spain were left mostly unsettled.

The castle wall of a Moorish palace and fortress, Calat Alhambra, the "red fortress," at Granada. One of Spain's architectural masterpieces, the magnificent Alhambra was the seat of Muslim rulers from the 13th century to the end of the 15th century.

AL-ANDALUS The independent Arab Muslim Umayyad dynasty of Spain ruled al-Andalus from 756 to 1031 from their capital at Córdoba. The reign of Caliph Abd-al-Rahmān III (912—961) marked the height of economic and cultural splendor in Muslim Spain. Al-Andalus became a region of intense trade, and its cities grew prosperous.

The Muslim rulers encouraged religious and cultural diversity. This meant that Christians and Jews were allowed to worship as they pleased but their status was that of *Dhimmis*, non-Muslims living in a land governed by Muslims. Christians and Jews had limited autonomy, full rights to practice their religion, and they were offered full protection by their Muslim rulers at a price. There was a specific tax called the *jizya* (zee-JAR) that Dhimmis had to pay. Those who did not pay the tax either converted to Islam or faced the death penalty. Al-Andalus was cultured and prosperous and European students traveled to Spain to learn Greek philosophy from the scholars there. Great strides were also made in astronomy, chemistry, and medicine.

A hand-colored woodcut of the Moors' surrender of Granada to Isabella and Ferdinand in 1492.

THE CHRISTIAN RECONQUEST

The Muslims allowed a few Christian territories to survive in the northern mountains, and these eventually grew into powerful kingdoms. The northern Christian kingdoms considered themselves the rightful lords of the peninsula and thus began the "reconquest" of Moorish Spain—the Christians were "reconquering" what they felt was rightfully theirs.

The regions of Navarre, Catalonia, Aragón, and Asturias became independent kingdoms by the 11th century, with Asturias, led by King Pelayo, becoming the most important driving force behind the Christian reconquest. By 1248 only Granada remained a Muslim territory. Muslim invasions from North Africa continued to threaten Christian Spain until the Christians finally took Granada in 1492. Spanish unity was settled by the end of the 15th century, although struggles for regional autonomy would persist.

THE CATHOLIC KINGS The two most important kingdoms in Spain were united in 1469 with the marriage of Isabella I, princess of Castile, and Ferdinand II, heir to the throne of Aragón. The Catholic kings, as the leaders of the two kingdoms were called, began their joint rule in 1479, and Isabella immediately took steps to centralize power.

In 1480 the Spanish Inquisition, authorized by a papal bull, was established. By 1492, with the last Moorish outpost conquered, all Jews and heretics (anyone who did not follow the orthodox teachings of the Catholic Church) were expelled from Spain. This threw the whole of Spain into a period of orthodox Catholicism that also spurred strong nationalist sentiments.

In 1492 the Italian explorer Christopher Columbus, sponsored by the Spanish Crown, sailed to the Americas and inspired a wave of Spanish exploration and conquest in the New World. Ferdinand and Isabella then turned their attention to acquiring other areas on the Iberian Peninsula and parts of Italy.

SPAIN DURING THE 16TH CENTURY

In 1516, following the deaths of Ferdinand and Isabella, their grandson Charles I assumed the throne of the joint kingdom, inaugurating Spain's Golden Age. In the 16th century Spain became the most powerful nation in the world, owing its immense wealth to its New World colonies and its alliance with the powerful Hapsburgs. The Hapsburg family dynasty originated in what is now Switzerland. They became the single most powerful family in Europe and provided rulers for several European states. The Hapsburgs wore the crown of the Holy Roman Empire from 1440 to 1806.

For the next two centuries, the fate of Spain was tied to the Hapsburg dynasty. In 1519 Charles I was elected Holy Roman emperor as Charles V and departed for Germany.

A statue of Columbus stands next to the waterfront of Port Vell in Barcelona.

THE HAPSBURG MONARCHS Charles I adopted his grandparents' ideals of Catholic unity and imperial conquests, which were financed by wealth from the New World. Following Columbus's voyages to the Americas, Hernán Cortés's conquest of Mexico's Aztec empire (1519—21) and Francisco Pizarro's conquest of the Incan empire in Peru (1531—33) brought even more riches from the New World. This wealth fueled the growth of cultural life in Spain and propelled the country into its Golden Age. Spanish artists, writers, and poets became increasingly accomplished and popular.

In 1556, with Spain's ever-increasing wealth causing inflation and a decrease in domestic industry, Charles I abdicated the throne in favor of his son, Philip II, who inherited the rule of Spain, Naples, Sicily, and the Netherlands. Philip II proceeded to lead the cause of the Counter-Reformation against Protestant states in Europe. The aim of the Counter-Reformation was to reform the Church and to establish and strengthen its traditions against the innovations of Protestant theology.

In 1588 he attempted to invade Protestant England by sea with his fleet, known until then as the "Invincible Armada," but was defeated. This defeat marked the beginning of the decline of Spanish power.

DECLINE OF SPANISH GLORY

By the end of the 16th century the economic and political glory of Spain had declined drastically, and the cultural leadership of Europe had passed to France. A series of weak kings and overly ambitious ministers contributed further to Spain's downfall. The Thirty Years' War (1618—48) began as a series of religious disputes that turned into a struggle between the Hapsburg and French Bourbon dynasties, each vying for control of Spain. This severely weakened Spain, and Hapsburg rule finally ended in Spain with the reign of Charles II (1665—1700).

THE SPANISH BOURBONS The 18th century began with the War of Spanish Succession (1701—14), by which French king Louis XIV acquired some Spanish territory and put his grandson, who became Philip V, on the Spanish throne. The early Bourbon rulers in Spain paid great attention to economic development and the centralization of power. By the mid-1700s Spain grew more prosperous and united, eventually becoming a union of provinces instead of the loose collection of kingdoms it had always been before.

With the introduction of rational and enlightened ideals, in part learned from France, Spain moved away from its strong religious orientation. By 1767 the Jesuits were expelled, and the powers of the Inquisition reduced. In later years Spain allied itself with France and was thus thrust into the Seven Years' War (1756—63) against Great Britain.

THE NAPOLEONIC PERIOD Spain's decline in subsequent years invited intervention by other powers, notably the French. In 1794, during France's revolutionary wars, Spain was made a French outpost. Resentment toward the Spanish throne and government grew, weakening Spain further.

This portrait of Ferdinand VII, king of Spain in 1808 and from 1813 to 1833, was painted by Francisco de Goya.

In 1808 Napoleon Bonaparte forced the king of Spain, Charles IV, to abdicate in favor of Napoleon's own brother Joseph Bonaparte. The Spaniards rebelled against French occupation and were eager to implement their own form of government. There were numerous local risings that met with success wherever French military power was weak.

Although a democratic constitution was drawn up, its progressive principles were disputed by the liberals and conservatives for about another 100 years. Through the efforts of a British army and Spanish guerrillas, France was forced to evacuate, and in 1814 the Spanish throne was restored with the return of Ferdinand VII, son of Charles IV.

After the French left, Spain was devastated by war and the loss of colonies in the New World. Although the rest of Europe was industrializing rapidly, Spain remained relatively undeveloped partly due to the moneyed classes' willingness to rely on agriculture. Economic stability, which would have allowed for industrial growth and development, was impeded for many decades.

PERIOD OF TROUBLES (1814—75) Internal conflicts ensued as efforts toward building a more liberal government were defeated by the autocratic Ferdinand VII. Quarrels over succession to the throne led to the Carlist Wars in 1833. The First Carlist War (1833—39) was fought in support of Don Carlos, a Bourbon traditionalist contender for the Spanish throne. Numerous military, peasant, and socialist uprisings as well as revolts of Carlists and federalists threatened to tear Spain apart. The instability of the government, which alternated between monarchy and republic for several years, added to the problems.

BOURBONS RESTORED The first Spanish Republic was declared in 1873, and in 1874 Alfonso XII, a Bourbon, became king. His reign from 1874 to 1875

The monument to Alfonso XII inside Retiro Park, Madrid.

was marked by free trade and gave rise to hopes for a stable constitutional monarchy in Spain. By 1890, however, with the declaration of universal suffrage for men, republicanism was again a growing force.

By 1897 the peaceful period had ended. A popular but conservative political leader, Antonio Cánovas del Castillo, was assassinated, and in 1898 Spain lost the last parts of its empire in the Americas and the Pacific—Cuba, Puerto Rico, the Philippines, Guam, and other islands—in the Spanish-American War.

Domestic problems, bitter war in northern Morocco, and increased unrest led to a military coup and the dictatorship of General Miguel Primo de Rivera in 1923. The general, who modeled his government on Italian fascism, was initially popular with the people, but his attacks on liberals and his economic mismanagement forced him to resign in 1930, leaving Spain in the hands of King Alfonso XIII. In 1931, following the election of a Republican-Socialist government, Alfonso abdicated and eventually left the country to avoid a civil war.

Nationalist leader General Francisco Franco overthrew the Spanish democratic republic in the Spanish Civil War.

REPUBLIC The Second Republic (1931—39) brought about increased political participation in Spain, but in so doing created its own set of conflicts. Spain became divided into two opposing factions: the right, the conservatives, and the left, the liberals. On the right were the military, the Church, landowners, and many small farmers, and on the left workers, landless peasants, intellectuals, and most Catalans and Basques. Some positive reforms were instituted during the first two years of the Republic, but eventually the disputes escalated into the Spanish Civil War (1936—39).

CIVIL WAR AND A NEW DICTATOR General Francisco Franco led the right-wing nationalist movement, aided by Italian and German fascists, and quickly conquered the western half of Spain. The Republicans, despite some Soviet aid, were weakened by internal divisions and eventually fell to Franco's army. The tragic war cost Spain hundreds of thousands of lives, and many Spaniards fled the country.

Franco ruled the devastated nation as a military dictator for the next 36 years, supported by the Catholic Church and the Falange—the official fascist state party. He proved to be a stern ruler. Although his regime began

Valle de los Caidos, or the Valley of the Fallen, commemorates the Civil War dead. Carved out of a mountain, it houses a basilica, a monastery, and General Franco's tomb. The top of the cross is 500 feet (152 m) above its granite base.

as a repressive, totalitarian system, Franco set up his own brand of fascism, unlike the German and Italian models.

Spain survived World War II by remaining officially neutral, as it had done during World War I, and this resulted in the Allies' negative feelings toward Spain.

AFTER FRANCO In 1947 Spain was declared a monarchy, with a king to be named to succeed Franco. In 1955 Spain became a member of the United Nations. Spain was still in a state of severe economic distress, and in the 1960s Franco took steps to liberalize the economy. In 1969 Franco named the exiled Prince Juan Carlos I de Borbón as his successor and heir to the vacant Spanish throne. After Franco's death in 1975, King Juan Carlos I, having sworn to uphold Francoist ideals while Franco was still alive, immediately started to initiate democratic reforms. He managed to guide Spain toward political liberalization with the help of the new prime minister, Adolfo Suárez González.

The first free general elections in 40 years were held in 1977. In 1978 a new constitution was put in place, restoring civil liberties and freedom of the press. In 1979 the parliament of Spain, the Cortes, approved provisional limited autonomy for Spain's regions, including Catalonia and the Basque provinces. Two attempted military coups, in 1981 and 1982, were easily suppressed. In 1981 King Juan Carlos made a television appearance to announce that he had ordered the armed forces to put down the coup. The rebel forces surrendered 22 hours after the coup had started. The 1982 coup was foiled at the planning stage. Spain suffered from continued unrest due mostly to terrorist activity from Basque separatists.

Spain's new government was very eager to create closer ties with other Western countries. Negotiations to join the European Community (EC) began in 1976 and culminated in Spain's entrance in 1986. Spain joined the North Atlantic Treaty Organization (NATO) in 1982. That same year, the

Socialist Party (Partido Socialista Obrero Español, or PSOE) won a majority in the national elections, and their leader Felipe González Márquez was sworn in as the prime minister. In 1993 González made history when he won an unprecedented fourth term as premier. José María Aznar López became prime minister in 1996, and was re-elected in 2000. José Luis Rodríguez Zapatero served as prime minister of Spain from 2004 until 2011. In July 2011, with Spain's economy floundering, Zapatero called an early election. In the general elections held on November 20, 2011, the Popular Party (PP) routed the PSOE, which turned in its worst performance since the post-Franco restoration of democracy. Zapatero remained prime minister of a caretaker administration until the formation of a new government by the conservative PP leader Mariano Rajoy in December 2011.

INTERNET LINKS

http://historyofislam.com/contents/the-classical-period/the-fall-of-granada/

This site provides detailed information on the causes and events leading up to the fall of Granada in 1492.

http://personales.ya.com/fororeal/infresp.htm

This website contains detailed information on the Spanish royal family, including photographs.

http://europeanhistory.about.com/od/spain/a/revoltcomun2.htm

This website on the Succession of 1516 provides information on the sequence of events that led Charles I, grandson of Ferdinand and Isabella, to accept the Spanish throne rather than acting as regent on behalf of his mother, Joanna.

www.bbc.co.uk/history/british/tudors/adams_armada_01.shtml

This website includes detailed information on the Spanish Armada.

In 1540 Saint Ignatius of Loyola founded the Jesuit religious order, and sparked the Counter-Reformation— a period of intense Catholic piety that was to dominate Spanish life for centuries.

GOVERNMENT

Spain's King Juan Carlos (*center left*), Queen Sofia (*center right*), Prince Felipe (*right of Queen Sofia*), and Princess Letizia (*right of Prince Felipe*) inside the Parliament building at the 10th constitutional legislature in Madrid on January 27, 2011.

3

SPAIN HAS COME A LONG WAY in becoming the democratic country it is today. In the 36 years of General Franco's military dictatorship, Spain suffered from restrictions on civil liberties and political activity, a repressed economy, and ostracism by most of the world.

Spain was not permitted to become a member of the United Nations until 1955 and of NATO until 1982. The 1950s and 1960s saw a relaxation of political and administrative controls, but only after persistent outcries for change.

Spain's government is a parliamentary democracy with a constitutional monarchy. This is similar to the system in Great Britain. The king is the head of state and represents Spain internationally, but he has no real constitutional powers in Spain.

Rebuilt in the mid-1700s, Madrid's Royal Palace is now used for state functions.

Juan Carlos I was born on January 5, 1938, and lived in exile until coming to Spain to be appointed monarch. He is the eldest son of Juan Carlos Teresa Silverio Alfonso de Borbón y Battenberg, Conde de Barcelona, popularly known as Don Juan, and Maria de las Mercedes de Borbón y Orleans. In an agreement between Don Juan and General Franco in 1954, Juan Carlos was given precedence as pretender to the Spanish throne.

In 1962 Prince Juan Carlos married Her Royal Highness Princess Sofía of Greece, eldest daughter of the late king Paul of the Hellenes and Queen Frederika of Greece. Today the king and queen of Spain, Juan Carlos and Sofía, have two daughters, HRH the Infanta Elena, born in 1963, and HRH the Infanta Cristina, born in 1965. Their son, HRH Prince Felipe, Prince of Asturias was born in 1968. On his 18th birthday in 1986, Felipe was formally invested as heir to the Spanish throne.

In 1969, having declared years before that Spain would be restored to a monarchy upon his death or retirement, Franco nominated Prince Juan Carlos I de Borbón, the grandson of the last reigning monarch, King Alfonso XIII, as heir to the throne. In November 1975, two days after Franco's death, the monarchy was reinstated, and Juan Carlos I was sworn in as king.

A NEW ERA FOR SPAIN

King Juan Carlos and his appointed prime minister Adolfo Suárez González moved energetically to reform and liberalize the political system. Political parties were legalized in 1976, and free general elections were held in 1977. In 1978 parliamentary democracy began with the adoption of a new constitution.

THE CONSTITUTION OF 1978

The constitution adopted in 1978, the eighth since 1812, was an important step for Spain in many ways. In particular it succeeded in sweeping away the repressive remains of the Franco regime.

Among other things, the constitution restored civil liberties and freedom of the press, speech, and association; abolished torture and the death penalty; extended the right to vote beyond family heads to all citizens over 18 years of age; disestablished Roman Catholicism as the official religion; and also paved the way for the reorganization and recognition of all provinces and their respective heritage. The Constitution of 1978 describes Spain as a hereditary, constitutional monarchy with a parliamentary form of government. Executive power rests with the king, prime minister, and Council of Ministers, or cabinet. However, the king plays a largely symbolic role in the entire system and has no real political authority.

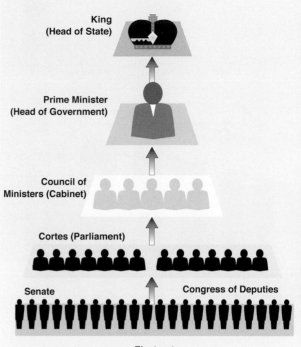

The Spanish system of government. Spain is a constitutional monarchy with a parliamentary form of government.

EXECUTIVE POWER

KING The king serves as head of state, commander-in-chief of the armed forces, and a symbol of Spain's unity and permanence. On the king's death or abdication, the crown passes to the eldest son, or if there is no male heir, to the eldest daughter.

The monarch exercises certain executive powers, drawing on the advice of the prime minister and Council of Ministers. Royal involvement in state affairs must be approved by the Cortes, the parliamentary assembly.

PRIME MINISTER Proposed by the king and elected by the legislature, the prime minister, or president, acts as head of the government, directing Spain's domestic, foreign, and military policies. First and second vice presidents are proposed by the prime minister and appointed by the king.

Mariano Rajoy is the incumbent prime minister. He is the leader of the conservative Popular Party (PP) and was elected in December 2011.

COUNCIL OF MINISTERS The Council of Ministers, or cabinet, is recommended by the prime minister and appointed by the king. The Council of Ministers assists the prime minister in running the country and reports to the lower house of the legislature, the Congress of Deputies, in matters of policy.

LEGISLATURE

Legislative power is invested in the parliamentary Cortes Generales, consisting of the very influential Congress of Deputies and the less powerful Senate. The Congress of Deputies has 350 members, elected proportionately according to the population of each province.

The Senate has 208 directly elected members and 49 regional representatives from the mainland and island provinces and from Ceuta and Melilla, the Spanish enclaves in Morocco. Elections are held for both the Congress of Deputies and the Senate every four years.

The neoclassical El Palacio del Congreso de los Diputados, or Spanish Congress of Deputies, in Madrid.

JUDICIARY

Spain's judicial system is headed by the Supreme Court, or Tribunal Supremo, and includes territorial, provincial, regional, and municipal courts. Each province has its own high court, which tries criminal cases.

The president of the Supreme Court, appointed by the king, also presides over the General Council of Judicial Power (CGPJ), formed by 20 members representing each facet of the judicial system—magistrates, judges, and attorneys. Members of the CGPJ have full judicial power independent of the executive and legislative branches and are appointed by the parliament and the king for five-year terms.

The Supreme Court is the highest authority in all questions of law, except constitutional issues, which the Constitutional Court handles. Consisting of 12 members appointed by the king for nine-year terms, the Constitutional Court is wholly responsible for the interpretation of the constitution: laws and regulations, violations of fundamental and individual rights, and conflicts between the state and autonomous regions. The jury system was established by the constitution in 1978.

REGIONAL GOVERNMENT

Spain is divided into 50 administrative provinces (including the Balearic and Canary islands), each with its own civil governor and elected local council that in turn elects mayors of cities and towns.

The Constitution of 1978 also provides for the establishment of 17 autonomous regions, including the provinces, in an effort to recognize, preserve, and respect the characteristics of each region. It was notably the strong demands of Basque and Catalan separatists that led to the creation of this system of regional self-government.

In 1979 the statutes of the first of the 17 Autonomous Communities were formalized, and the first parliaments were elected in the Basque Country and Catalonia in 1980, followed by Galicia in 1981 and Andalusia in 1982. By 1983 the process was completed throughout all remaining 13 regions.

These regional governing bodies operate within the framework of Spain's constitution and national laws and policies. Certain important powers are delegated to them, such as the election of regional legislatures and presidents, management of land use, public works and transportation, agricultural development, tourism, social and health aid, and the right to speak different languages and practice different cultural traditions.

INTERNET LINKS

www.spartacus.schoolnet.co.uk/2WWfranco.htm

This website provides a detailed biography of the famous Spanish dictator Francisco Franco.

www.indexmundi.com/spain/government_profile.html

This website provides detailed information on the government of Spain.

www.bbc.co.uk/news/world-europe-15781440

This site contains a profile of Spain's prime minister and leader of the conservative Popular Party, Mariano Rajoy.

ECONOMY

Modern skyscrapers adorn the business district of Madrid.

4

FOR MANY YEARS SPAIN'S ECONOMY lagged behind that of its Western European neighbors. Having been relatively slow to industrialize during the 18th and 19th centuries—periods of great industrial growth in other countries—Spain's economy remained agriculture-based through the first half of the 20th century.

The Spanish Civil War brought about widespread devastation and great loss of life. A period of isolation and economic depression followed. In the late 1950s Franco attempted to make Spain more self-sufficient by reducing foreign imports and expanding domestic industry. Today Spain's economy is closely tied to its global trade partners.

The port of Barcelona is Spain's major Mediterranean port and commercial center.

The international financial crisis and its consequences for the global economy have definitively altered the Spanish economy. Facing a recession in 2012, Spain introduced austerity measures of social and economic reforms aimed to reduce unemployment and combat tax fraud.

ECONOMIC RESCUE EFFORTS

The state-run National Industrial Institute (INI), set up to supplement private investment in areas of national interest, turned out to be a wasteful enterprise that encouraged inefficient industry practices and caused high inflation rates. In 1959 Franco implemented a stabilization program that marked a turning point in Spain's economy, liberalizing trade and foreign investment. Spain made strong progress with a series of economic development plans, but per capita income was still far below that in many European nations. Spain, like many other countries, was hard hit by the oil price increases of 1973 and 1979. Many industries suffered during the late 1970s and early 1980s when industrial output growth remained at a low of only one percent.

Factories with modern equipment, such as this fruit packaging plant, enable Spain to compete with other industrialized nations.

Perhaps the single most profound addition to Spain's economic improvement plan was the country's admission in 1986 to the European Community (which in 1993 became the European Union). This helped sustain Spain's economic growth for several years, until 1991 when the country experienced high inflation rates. By early 1993 Spain's economy was in recession; recovery the following year was slow. Unemployment was a serious problem, affecting 18.4 percent of the labor force. Spain gained admission to the first group of countries launching the European single currency, the euro, in January 1999. Spain's unemployment rate fell but rose sharply to 26 percent in April 2013.

MANUFACTURING AND MINING

About 30.1 percent of Spain's labor force is employed in manufacturing, mining, and construction, which contribute roughly 26 percent of the gross domestic product (GDP). Basic industries, such as iron and steel, shipbuilding, machine tools, and metallurgy, are located in the north of

In 1950 Spain was a devastatingly poor country, weakened by the Civil War, poor agricultural production, and isolation from foreign investment. In 1953 Franco signed a pact with the United States, granting U.S. forces the right to establish military bases on Spanish soil in exchange for foreign aid and arms. The economic effects of this agreement were far-reaching, and indeed turned the tide.

U.S. military and civilian personnel poured into Spain, and with them came American dollars and tourists. Spain at long last had the funds necessary to rebuild its crumbling economy. In 1955 Spain was accepted into the United Nations, thereby attracting more foreign investment. Franco's Stabilization Plan of 1959, a move that increased domestic productivity and efficiency and liberalized foreign trade, readied Spain even more for the economic boom that was to come in the 1960s.

High industrial growth rates led to the creation of a new and prosperous middle class and brought financial stability to the working class.

Spain in Bilbao, Santander, and Oviedo. Equally important are manufacturing industries such as plastics, rubber, textiles, and electronics, located in Catalonia. A small concentration of industry occurs in Madrid, generally light chemical industry and high technology. Leather goods and shoes are produced in the Alicante province and in the Balearic Islands, and toys in Barcelona. Spain is also a large exporter of automobiles, but is facing increased competition from Poland and Turkey.

The most valuable metals and minerals mined are gold, zinc, copper, mercury, anthracite, coal, lignite, sulfur, potassium, fluorspar, and lead. Both natural gas and crude petroleum are produced in small quantities. To lessen Spain's dependence on imported oil, the use of alternative sources of energy has increased dramatically in the past decade. In fact, nuclear power provided 15 percent of Spain's electricity in 2009, and hydroelectricity provided 25 percent.

The Riotinto mine in Andalusia was once the world's largest copper producer but has been closed since 2001.

AGRICULTURE

The importance of agriculture to the Spanish economy has declined in recent decades. In 1950 more than half of Spain's labor force was employed in agriculture, compared with about 4.2 percent today. Agriculture now contributes only about 3.3 percent to the GDP annually. About a third of the country's land is cultivated, with grain—most notably wheat and barley—occupying more than 60 percent of the cultivated area. Olive groves and vineyards also cover large areas, making Spain the world's largest producer of olive products and third-largest producer of wine. Other crops important to the economy are citrus fruit, vegetables, rice, sugar beets, cotton, and tobacco.

Spain's rough, irregular terrain and meager rainfall have resulted in low agricultural productivity. Irrigation, used extensively in drier regions, and technological advances in cultivation are helping to create more diversified farming. Livestock production is generally weak in Spain, although 25.2 percent of the cultivated land is used as pastureland. Sheep and pigs are the two most important animals raised for meat.

FISHING AND FORESTRY

Fishing has always been a significant industry for Spain. The country has one of the largest fishing fleets in the world. The main fishing region is in

Groves of olive trees cover this fertile valley in Andalusia.

the northwest, off the coast of Galicia. Hake, anchovies, tuna, sardines, and cod are important catches, along with various mollusks and crustaceans.

Spain also has 71,454 square miles (185,066 square km) of forest. Lumber, cork, resin, and Spanish hemp are the leading forest products.

TOURISM

The tourist industry is a major source of revenue for Spain, the third most visited country in the world after France and the United States. In 2012 Spain welcomed just under 58 million tourists. This figure is even more amazing if compared with Spanish demographics: in 2012 Spain had a population of 47,042,984 people. Most tourists visit places along the Mediterranean coast. A large number of these visitors are from France, Portugal, Germany, Britain, and Morocco. Spain's nature conservation programs also attract a large number of avid eco-tourists every year.

FOREIGN INVESTMENT AND TRADE

Foreign investment has made very important contributions to Spain's economy and industrialization process. In the automobile industry, for example, investments by the U.S. companies Ford and General Motors in the areas of Valencia, Saragossa, and Cádiz have helped make Spain the ninth-largest exporter of cars in the world. The automobile industry in Spain accounts for 7 percent of all industrial employment and 5 percent of gross domestic product. Volkswagen, a German corporation, purchased SEAT, the Spanish automobile manufacturer, from the government. Today SEAT is Spain's largest producer of automobiles and employs the greatest number of workers.

Spain's major trading partners within the EU are Germany, France, Portugal, Italy, and the United Kingdom. Outside of Europe, the largest and most important trading partner is the United States. Spain also trades with

Originating from Santander, Spain, Banco Santander is the largest bank in the Eurozone and one of the largest banks in the world. It was ranked the sixth-largest company in the world by *Forbes Magazine Global* in 2010. By 2012, it fell to 23rd place.

Japan. Its main imports are petroleum products and mineral fuels, machinery, foodstuffs, consumer goods, and electrical equipment. Exports include automobiles, grain, fruit and vegetable products, olive oil, wine, metals, and textiles and apparel (including shoes).

THE SPANISH WORKDAY

The Spanish workday begins at 9:00 A.M., Monday through Saturday, although some businesses are closed all day Saturday.

An architect and an engineer on a construction site. More than nine out of every 10 Spaniards live and work in cities and towns.

Most businesspeople work until 1:30 P.M., and it is common to fill the morning hours with appointments and calls. Lunchtime is at 2:00 P.M., and the Spanish lunch is a leisurely one, whether it surrounds a business occasion or not. Siesta, an afternoon nap or rest, is traditional in Spain and is taken after a hearty midday meal. Many businesses close between 1:00 and 4:00 P.M. to accommodate this lull in the day. Most Spaniards then return to their offices, where they continue working until 8:00 or 9:00 P.M.

Spanish businesspeople can be somewhat conservative, and they take their work seriously. They invariably show respect for a person of higher rank or position and will hardly argue or voice any disagreement in direct language, as honor takes precedence over all else.

Women working in offices typically wear tailored dresses or blouses and skirts. Men tend to wear jackets and ties, no matter how high the temperature is outside.

Although Spaniards are formal and reserved about dress, position, and integrity, they can be much more casual about time. Although punctuality is taken as a sign of seriousness, purpose, or reliability, running a few minutes late is acceptable and considered unavoidably human; being angered by a short delay would seem ridiculously exaggerated.

It is also not the Spanish way to discuss business at the first meeting. The initial introduction is more an opportunity for both parties to get to know each other. In general, business contacts are more readily cultivated among friends.

CURRENT TRENDS

In 2007 Spain's economy grew by 3.5 percent and the public account surplus was more than 2 percent of gross domestic product, largely due to a construction boom. By 2008 the property bubble burst, the surplus became a deficit, and economic growth fell to 0.9 percent. By 2013 Spain's unemployment rate was over 26 percent, the highest it's been in many generations, with a record 5.8 million people unemployed. Spain's cabinet approved a labor market reform, which was criticized by unions as undermining workers' rights.

Austerity measures were introduced, including an increase in VAT, an increase in the tax on tobacco, and slashes in wind power subsidies. Pension reforms were passed to raise the retirement age to 67 from 65. In June 2001 Zapatero called an early election and in November 2011 Mariano Rajoy's center-right Popular Party won an absolute majority as voters showed their dissatisfaction at the outgoing Socialist government for the worst economic crisis in generations and the highest unemployment rate in the EU. Further austerity measures were announced in December 2011 as Spain faced its worst financial crises. Another recession is anticipated, which is expected to last at least another two years.

In 2012, Spain's GDP was estimated at $1.407 trillion, and in 2013, inflation was at 1.4 percent and the unemployment rate at 26.7 percent.

INTERNET LINKS

http://minerals.usgs.gov/minerals/pubs/country/2009/myb3-2009-sp.pdf

This site contains detailed information on the mineral industry of Spain, including government policies, programs, and statistics.

www.tradingeconomics.com/spain/forest-area-sq-km-wb-data.html

This website provides statistics and other qualitative information on land use in Spain.

http://www.spain.info/en/

This site includes interesting tourism information on Spain.

ENVIRONMENT

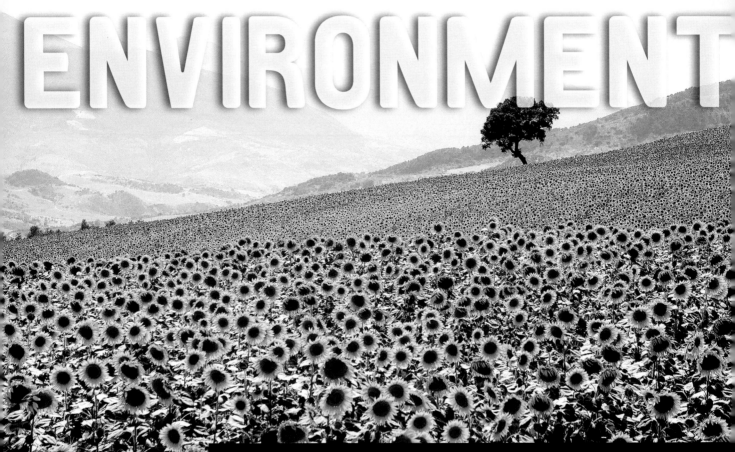

A bright patch of sunflowers fills this field in Andalusia. Andalusia boasts several UNESCO World Heritage sites: in Granada, the Alhambra palace, the Generalife gardens and the medieval Albaicín neighbourhood; in Córdoba, its historic center with the great Mosque; in Seville, the cathedral, the Alcázar palace and the Indies Archive; and in Jaén, the monumental sites of Úbeda and Baeza.

5

S IMILAR TO MOST EUROPEAN
countries, Spain faces a number of
environmental challenges. Big cities
such as Madrid, Barcelona, and Gerona
suffer pollution from motor vehicle
emissions and industrial waste, while large
tracts of agricultural land are being lost to
urbanization and new highways. Areas on
the Mediterranean coast suffer pollution
from raw sewage and effluents from the
offshore production of oil and gas.

An aerial view of the Mequinenza Dam (which created a lake called the Aragon Sea)
along the Ebro River. Huge catfish, larger than a man, have been caught here.

The construction
boom in Spain has
caused considerable
impact on the
environment. In
2010 Greenpeace
stated that 19 acres
(7.7 hectares) of
coastline per day
are being
destroyed for
urban, commercial, or
industrial purposes.
This construction
activity, whether
on the coast or
inland, has negative
environmental
effects on wildlife,
water quality
and availability, and
Spain's overall
natural beauty.

The Sunstroom solar power farm complex at Los Arcos, Navarra. Apart from on these farms, solar panels are commonly used to generate energy for residential homes.

More and more Spaniards are developing an interest in protecting the environment and preventing urban development from encroaching on nature spots. In one coastal village, the inhabitants circulated a petition to stop the construction of a large marina, which would have ruined the natural beauty of the coastline.

Aware of the need to prevent further deterioration of the environment, the Spanish government is now party to a number of international agreements that address pressing environmental issues.

Some areas of focus include air pollution, biodiversity, climate change, endangered species, hazardous waste, and marine dumping. The use of alternative energy is also widely encouraged, with solar panels and aerogenerators becoming an increasingly common sight all around the country.

NATURAL WEALTH

The estimated annual cost of desertification in Spain due to climate change, poor land use, and the overuse of water resources is $200 million.

Spain covers close to three-quarters of the entire Iberian Peninsula on which it is located. This large area means it also spans a variety of climatic zones and ecosystems.

Green Spain in the far north experiences plentiful rainfall and produces vegetation of a most intense shade of green. Inland Spain, on the other hand, is where the bright sunlight on the Meseta can hurt your eyes, and temperatures are known to soar in summer and plummet in winter. The rugged mountain ranges of the Pyrenees, along the fertile coastal plains of the eastern seaboard, were painstakingly carved into hillside terraces by the Moors. In southern Spain the dry desert-like landscapes around the coastal town of Almería have often been used as locations for filming spaghetti westerns, Italian-produced westerns.

NATURAL HAZARDS

Drought in some parts of Spain causes the earth to harden so that when rain does finally fall, it cannot soak into the soil. Instead it gushes down hillsides and through coastal villages where adequate drains are rare. Flash floods caused by continuous torrential rainfall have been known to sweep cars off the streets and drown people and animals.

Mudcracks in Coto Doñana, Andalusia, one of the most important wetland wildlife sites in Europe. The important lagoons have regressed by 70 percent due to overabstraction of ground water for the tourist resort industry in Huelva.

New housing developments contribute to water problems. Because the coastal plains are popular with foreigners seeking the ideal retirement home, many vineyards, citrus and almond orchards, and olive groves in these areas have been replaced by modern roads and buildings. Even in a relatively small coastal town like Benitachell in Alicante province, most houses have swimming pools. Water rationing is a necessary measure to control consumption.

Drought can also lead to forest fires, especially during the summer months. This is indeed a huge concern as forests already cover just over half of Spain's land area. In some cases the fires are deliberate. Permission has to be obtained before trees can be cut down, even in one's own garden, so fires may be started on purpose in locations where developers wish to build villas. Once the land is cleared of trees, permission to build may be granted

Insufficient rainfall creates droughts in many coastal and southern regions of Spain. Supplying towns and villages with decent potable water throughout the year is a major challenge. Salty water, water rationing, and frequent cuts in water supply have caused a drop in the number of summer tourists. As a result many towns in tourist areas have had to install desalination plants. However, desalination plants are expensive to run.

With four filtration units, each purifying 229,545 cubic feet (6,500 cubic m) of water every 24 hours, a plant needs 6,000 watts of electricity. First a number of wells must be expertly drilled to a depth of 656 feet (200 m) approximately 984 feet (300 m) from the sea. The seawater is partially purified as it filters through earth on its way inland to the wells. Water from the wells is pumped into sand-filter tanks in the desalination plant and then through a series of increasingly fine filters until it is purified. This filtration process is called "reverse osmosis." The heavy metals extracted during the purification process must be carefully disposed of. To reduce the salinity of the effluent, 40 percent of the water that is processed is mixed with four parts of normal seawater and dumped back into the sea.

more readily. The Spanish government tries to repair damage caused by forest fires by planting new trees as part of its reforestation programs, and each province has a District Forest Office in charge of all forestry matters.

Various research institutions are actively involved in proposing more effective solutions for responding to natural hazards. One such body is the Center for Forest Technology located in Catalonia, which engages scientists to collate factual and scientific knowledge in order to help policymakers establish appropriate programs. The industry most affected by natural hazards is agriculture. Earthquakes and other natural hazards account for more than half of all damage caused to crops and agricultural land. Essential infrastructure like power plants and roads are also vulnerable, and damages to these are most expensive to repair. In October 2011 two earthquakes struck close to the town of Lorca in the Murcia region of southeast Spain, killing 10 people.

A view of the interior of Tenerife, Canary Islands showing new trees being planted in the lava ash as part of reforestation efforts in Spain.

ENDANGERED SPECIES

The dense forests and grazing lands of Green Spain and the Pyrenees provide a perfect environment for mountain animals. Until recently hunting was a popular sport that drove some species close to extinction.

Following government initiatives, hunting is strictly controlled today, and vast areas in Spain have been set aside as national parks, nature reserves, and bird sanctuaries. In the mountains near Madrid, for example, wolves have been protected for decades by a government ban on hunting them. The measure proved successful, as wolves have populated the area again. However, farmers are not pleased because the ban also prevents them from

IBERIAN LYNX

*The Iberian lynx (*Lynx pardinus*) is the world's most endangered cat. Driven to the edge of extinction by loss of prey, habitat destruction, and trapping, 10 years ago there were barely 100 Iberian lynxes left. In 2003 an innovative Spanish conservation program, the Lynx Life Project, was established in Olivilla, Andalucia, to provide shelter for 32 lynxes in 20 enclosures, with each cat's behavior being monitored round-the-clock by dozens of ecologists, vets, and other staff. Since then the animal's population has risen to more than 300, and some have been released back into the wild.*

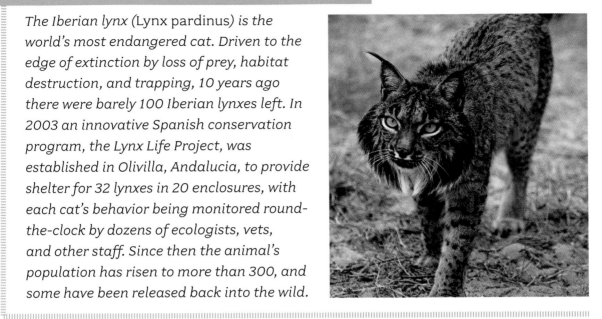

killing wolves that raid their properties. Since each shepherd can lose as many as 40 sheep in a night, the regional authorities have had to introduce compensation schemes to mitigate opposition from farmers.

Within Alicante's provincial district of Marina Alta, the mountains provide a habitat for a variety of animals such as rabbits, weasels, foxes, boars, badgers, squirrels, and mountain cats. The highest mountain in this area is the Aitana at 5,108 feet (1,557 m). Birds of prey such as goshawks, tawny owls, eagles, sparrowhawks, and falcons glide freely over this region, which provides nesting grounds for barn owls, crows, ravens, rooks, thrushes, robins, blackbirds, swifts, and swallows.

Significant efforts are being made to protect such areas. The Pego-Oliva Marsh Nature Park, for instance, provides a nature reserve and bird sanctuary. Its main roads lead inland where the plains are carpeted with shrubs like mastic, rosemary, and thyme, and dotted with pines, olive trees, carob, and almond trees. Similarly, in the southwest, the Doñana National Park is famous for its wildlife, and conservation initiatives are in place to ensure that many species are protected.

The Spanish imperial eagle (*Aquila adalberti*) has recovered spectacularly over the past 30 years, and is one of the success stories of conservation in Spain. The eagle population has increased from 38 pairs in 1974 to 253 pairs in 2008.

A row of recycling bins in Catalonia.

ALTERNATIVE ENERGY

Alternative energy is also quickly gaining popularity. Solar panels are common on the rooftops of modern villas and are also used to heat swimming pools. Vast banks of aerogenerators exist in areas where there are strong winds. Even remote villages have set up bottle banks for recycling, with special containers to collect paper and clothing.

These days even remote villages participate in recycling efforts. Children are educated on such environmental concerns from an early age.

INTERNET LINKS

www.iberianature.com/

This site is a guide to the Iberian environment, climate, wildlife geography, and nature of Spain, and a source of up-to-date information on Spanish flora and fauna.

www.technologyreview.com/microsites/spain/water/index.aspx

Spain built Europe's first desalination plant nearly 40 years ago. This website provides information on the history of desalination, environmental challenges, and the increase in desalination plants in Spain and around the world.

SPANIARDS

Women dressed in traditional Spanish outfits in Andalusia.

6

SPAIN HAS A POPULATION of roughly 47.5 million, distributed unevenly around the country. Traditionally a rural, agricultural society, Spain has made the transition to an urban, industrialized nation.

Since the 1950s more than 5 million Spaniards have left the predominantly impoverished rural regions and small towns of the west and south for the more industrial cities, such as Madrid, Barcelona, and Bilbao. A significant number have also left Spain to take up jobs in more prosperous countries in Western Europe, such as the United Kingdom, Switzerland, France, and Germany. In 2013, with youth unemployment at unprecedentedly high levels of around 56 percent, a report from the Eurobarometer revealed that almost 70 percent of young Spanish people are thinking of going abroad to look for work. The Eurobarometer was established in 1973. It is a series of surveys carried out on behalf of the European Commission to measure public opinion.

A modern Spanish family enjoying a picnic in Mallorca.

The location of Spain, in Europe but close to Africa, has resulted in a large ethnic diversity and the mixing of many races and cultures over the years. Distinct ethnic groups within Spain include the Basques, Catalans, and Galicians. Spain is overwhelmingly urban, with 76 percent of its people living in towns and cities.

Spaniards come from diverse ethnic and linguistic groups whose struggles for recognition have sometimes been disruptive to society. In many instances a Spaniard's loyalty is first to his or her *patria chica* (PAH-tree-ya CHEE-kah), or native region, and then to the country. It has not been easy for the government to recognize these differences and loyalties, however. Repressed during much of the Franco years, regional communities were only granted more recognition in the Constitution of 1978, which guarantees autonomy for the diverse nationalities that make up Spain. Although Castilian Spanish is still the official language, the constitution recognizes the distinct local languages such as Catalan, Galician, and Euskera and declares them co-official with Castilian Spanish for governmental purposes.

Elderly men sitting on a park bench in La Seu d'Urgell, Catalonia.

THE PRINCIPAL ETHNIC GROUPS

The principal ethnic groups are: Catalans, representing 17 percent of the population; Basques, making up 2 percent; and Galicians, or *Gallegos* (gah-YEH-gohs), representing 7 percent. Other groups include the Valencians, Navarrese, Aragónese, and Roma.

THE CATALANS The region of Catalonia, including the provinces of Barcelona, Lérida, Tarragona, and Gerona, is the homeland of the Catalans. There are also Catalan-speaking communities in the Balearic Islands, parts of Valencia, and Aragón.

The site of many invasions and wars in the past, Catalonia has a rich history. The region became part of a united Spain during the reign of Ferdinand and Isabella. Hundreds of years later, during the Spanish Civil War, there existed for a short time a proud "Catalan Republic," which also served as a base for many of the era's anarchists and communists.

Although the independent republic did not survive the Franco years, autonomy for this region has never ceased to be an issue, and the Catalans are second only to the Basques in their persistence for recognition.

The latter part of the 19th century saw renewed cultural pride and a sort of renaissance for the Catalans. Several criteria were used to distinguish the Catalans from other Spaniards. Loyalty to Catalonia and its culture was probably the most important, along with the ability to speak the language. What began in the last century continues today, with emphasis on the Catalan language itself as the key to cultural distinctiveness.

The educational policy of the region is that all students should be bilingual in Catalan and Castilian. However, more subjects are taught in Catalan than in Castilian.

The Catalan region is prosperous, industrialized, and thoroughly urbanized, and Catalans are on the whole noted for their business sense, entrepreneurial skills, and thrift.

A Basque with the ubiquitous beret.

THE BASQUES Basque is a language with no known linguistic relatives spoken by about 660,000 people mainly in the Basque country (Euskal Herria) in the north of Spain and the southwest of France. In Spain the Basque country incorporates the provinces of Álava, Vizcaya, and Guipúzcoa. No one is certain how the Basques came to settle in this remote region of Spain, but they are clearly among the earliest people to inhabit Europe. The Basques are by nature a fiercely independent people, proud of their own rural culture and their difficult, mysterious language called Euskera (yoo-SKAY-rah), an isolate that has not been shown conclusively to be related to any other language.

Basques were great warriors. By the Middle Ages the Basques were still largely untouched by the rest of European history and activity. Integrated into the kingdom of Castile in the 16th century, the Basques still managed to retain some privileges and exemptions by virtue of their cultural uniqueness.

In the 20th century Franco made great efforts to repress Basque culture, especially their language. This was fiercely opposed by the Basque people, and today the Basque spirit of defiance lives on. The worst example of this defiance is terrorist violence by Euskadi Ta Askatsuna (ETA), a Basque nationalist and separatist organization fighting for total independence from the Spanish government. Nevertheless the Basque region is one of the most prosperous in Spain. Its metal, steel, and shipbuilding industries continue to attract migrant workers from the inland and southern regions of Spain.

THE GALICIANS The provinces of La Coruña, Lugo, Orense, and Pontevedra make up the region of Galicia in the northwestern corner of Spain. Galicians are descended from early Celtic invaders who came from northern Europe and settled in Galicia between 1000 B.C. and 600 B.C. In the 20th century almost a million people migrated out of Galicia to seek their fortunes in Spain's urban centers. The region is sparsely populated and quite rural, and there is no real industry.

In the middle of the 19th century Galician nationalism was built around a nostalgic tale of the region's Golden Age during the Middle Ages. Although such a kingdom did exist, it was rather short-lived. The southern part of the kingdom eventually became Portugal, while the northern portion was in complete disorder until 1483 when it was incorporated into the kingdom of Castile.

Modern-day nationalist movements date from 1931, but in general Galician efforts for autonomy are more moderate in comparison with the aggressive demands of both the Catalans and the Basques.

Almost 60 percent of Galicia's population can claim authentic Galician ethnicity. Many still use the Galician language and it is studied at school. The language is also more widely used in rural communities than in urban centers.

Galicians are by trade and tradition fishermen, shepherds, and farmers. Many of them still have not achieved the wealth and education of those living in the cities.

A farmer in Galicia. Galicians have more of a Celtic heritage than other Spaniards and are noted for their blond hair and light-colored eyes.

ROMA

Roma are a small ethnic group in Spain, and their origins are generally unknown. It is thought that they migrated from Iran or India to Europe as early as the 11th century, arriving in Spain as early as the 15th century. No one really knows how many Roma live in Spain today; their nomadic lifestyle makes it difficult to conduct a census of their population. It is estimated that up to 970,000 Roma live in Spain, which is about 2 percent of the world Roma population. When they settled in Spain in the 1400s, it is believed that the Roma were rather well received. However, circumstances changed during the Spanish Inquisition when the Roma, along with the Moors and the Jews, were either driven out of Spain or forced to assimilate. Under Franco, their persecution continued, and they were still considered an underclass in the 1980s.

Roma women carry baskets of laundry on the shores of the Guadalquivir River in Spain.

Recent programs, however, have promoted education in Roma communities to bring them into mainstream Spanish and European society. Care is also taken not to eliminate their rich and distinctive cultural traditions in the process. In particular, their passionate music and dance have charmed audiences worldwide.

Spanish Roma are divided into two groups. The *gitanos* (hee-TAH-nos) generally live in southern and central Spain, and most make a living as street entertainers or vendors. The *húngaros* (OONG-gah-ros) come from central Europe, are generally poorer than the *gitanos*, and live a more nomadic lifestyle, pitching temporary tents and shacks on the city fringes. In Spain only 5 percent of Roma live in makeshift camps, and about half are homeowners.

CLASS STRUCTURE

Class structure and social hierarchies are changing in Spain as the country becomes more industrialized. Like Spain's Western European neighbors, Spanish society is increasingly differentiated along occupational and professional lines.

A young girl wears the traditional outfit in Salamanca.

The upper class consists of wealthy professionals and big landowners, roughly 13 percent of the population. The middle class, which includes technical professionals, small business owners, and mid-level public and private employees, makes up 36.3 percent of the population. The lower class—16.5 percent of the population—consists of lower-skilled workers and farmers. Spain's middle class is expanding, while the number of rural poor is decreasing. Education is a principal vehicle for mobility after family eminence and some level of inherited wealth.

In the small villages of the Meseta and the north, where most inhabitants own land that they themselves work, there are fewer differences in class and status. There are still many large landholders dominating the countryside. People are less likely to be classified according to jobs and monetary earnings and more likely to feel bound to one another by religion and kinship.

As modernization transforms these villages, the gaps in material possessions between rich and poor are also less obvious. One person is just as likely to own a car, television, or refrigerator as any other. However, this sense of community is not the case in the agricultural towns of Andalusia. Large expanses of land are owned by relatively few owners. This *latifundio*, or large estate, system is notable for two regressive characteristics: unproductive use of the land, and unequal and absentee landownership patterns. A tiny percent of the agricultural population owns more than half of the land. The workers of this land are mainly landless day laborers, called *jornaleros* (HOR-nah-LEH-ros), who do not even live on the land but in "agro-towns" with populations of up to 30,000. These agro-towns are inhabited almost solely by day laborers. Class delineation between the landowners and the day laborers is still sharply evident.

DRESS

Spaniards today dress much like other Western Europeans and North Americans. There was a time when Spanish women wore heavy black clothes, but now only the older generation in rural areas dresses this way.

Certain areas of Spain, such as Madrid, Barcelona, Valencia, and Málaga, are becoming more fashion conscious and the more stylish inhabitants of these cities can match the dress sense of any chic Parisian or American. For most other Spaniards, conservative dress is the norm. Office workers and professionals wear general business attire. Students wear jeans, baggy sweaters, and whatever else attracts their eye, just as students in other Western cultures do. Agricultural and factory workers dress to suit the physical requirements of their work. Shorts are not worn in public much, except by tourists in beach and resort areas.

Spanish college students in casual attire.

INTERNET LINKS

http://spanish.about.com/od/spanishlanguageculture/a/spainlanguages.htm

This site on Spain's linguistic diversity provides information and examples of the Euskera and Catalan languages spoken in Spain.

www.turgalicia.es/portada?langId=en_US

This informative site contains images and video clips, showing Galician landscapes, cityscapes, architecture, and cultural traditions with musical clips and quotes from poets and writers.

www.time.com/time/world/article/0,8599,2019316,00.html

This site is about the Gypsies of Spain and how their lives have improved dramatically since the dictator Francisco Franco died.

www.everyculture.com/Sa-Th/Spain.html#b

This website includes detailed information about the culture of Spain illustrated with interesting old black-and-white photographs.

Living conditions have improved dramatically over the past few years. There are now 19.9 million main line telephones, 52.5 million mobile (cell) phones, and 28.11 million Internet users in Spain.

Shoppers resting at a coffee joint in La Canada shopping center in Marbella.

7

AS VARIED AS SPANIARDS ARE IN ethnicity and lifestyle, there still exists a distinct, national personality that links the different peoples and cultures of Spain.

Spaniards are generally vivacious, ready to enjoy a party and join in celebrations. They are passionate about the arts, their family, and their faith. At the same time, they never fail to enjoy modest pleasures: a good meal, a sunny courtyard filled with flowering plants, the company of friends, a relaxing siesta, and a hearty laugh—these are the makings of Spanish life.

Families waiting excitedly for a parade in Granada.

The Spanish culture and lifestyle is a result of geographical location and is widely sprinkled with the influence of other cultures. These influences range from Iberic, Phoenician, and Roman to Greek and North African.

A wedding group poses for a shot on the steps of a church in Catalonia.

SOCIAL CUSTOMS

Spaniards are at ease with themselves and their world, but they do adhere to certain social graces. Invitations to the homes of friends are considered an honor, as Spaniards generally open their homes only to family and very close friends. Guests rarely refuse invitations (to do so without just cause would be an insult), and they bring with them flowers, sweets, or gifts for the little children.

Spaniards greet with affection and warmth. Men and women kiss on each cheek when they meet. In more formal settings, men shake hands when they greet and again on departing. Spaniards consider small talk superficial and impersonal, and they often express their strongly held opinions very frankly and directly, even on the first meeting.

Recognition of rank is taken for granted in Spain, whether in the home, the office, or everyday life. Children do not openly defy or show disrespect to their parents by talking back or disobeying in public. Likewise in business, bosses or supervisors are treated with respect even when they falter; errors or embarrassments are never pointed out by a subordinate. Compared to the world of business in some other Western cultures, in Spain respect for one's superiors supersedes personal ambition.

Religion, politics, and affairs of the heart are subjects of discussion generally avoided until a more intimate relationship develops between the parties involved.

In the past, when the lines between rich and poor were more sharply delineated, the opinions and actions of a wealthy landowner or official had terrific sway over those of a poor laborer or member of the rural lower class. As the middle class grows in Spain today—and it will continue to do so with the government's far-reaching economic policies—these lines of social distinction are becoming more and more blurred.

No longer does a poor person automatically defer to someone who is rich. By constitutional decree, each Spaniard has an equal right to all that society has to offer: political voice, economic opportunities, education, and recreation.

SPANISH PRIDE

Spanish pride is legendary. Where else in the world would an opportunistic warrior (El Cid) be a national hero and a fictitious half-crazed dreamer (Don Quixote) be a symbol of the noble cause? Where would people cheer a dying bull for fighting bravely in the ring and boo the victorious matador who did not? The essence of the Spanish character lies in their honor, their sense of dignity, and their adherence to what they believe to be morally right and wrong.

The monument to Cervantes in Plaza de España in Madrid features Don Quixote riding his horse, Rocinante, and Sancho Panza riding his donkey. These heroes epitomize the Spanish culture of taking pride in all that they do.

These principles are still evident today, as Spaniards continue to take themselves and their efforts seriously. Spaniards take pride in their birthplace, their region, and their culture. These elements underlie the regional separatist movements that have been around for centuries, especially those of the Catalans and Basques. In these regions, efforts are widespread to restore the use of regional languages in schools, on public signs, and at home and to pass on cultural traditions to the next generation.

A Spanish man takes pride in being a good father, husband, and provider. A Spanish woman keeps a clean house, makes sure the children are well taken care of and healthy, and goes to work with efficiency and poise.

EL CID: THE NATIONAL HERO

Ruy Díaz de Vivar, known as El Cid (derived from the Arabic word sidi, *meaning "leader" or "lord"), was born in the town of Burgos in 1043. This historical figure was a warrior of questionable loyalty, but his victories made him famous. He fought against both Christians and Moors as it suited him, but his greatest triumphs were over the Moors. In 1094 El Cid captured Valencia from the Muslims and ruled there until his death five years later.*

His exploits were made legendary in the Spanish epic The Poem of the Cid, *written by an anonymous monk just 40 years after El Cid died. The poem deserves to be read*

for its faithful portrayal of the manners and customs of the day.

El Cid will always be remembered for his dignity and courage. He fought and went to war for the sheer glory of it all and was victorious because of his own will and belief in himself. Many towns all over Spain still bear his name.

It is said that a Spaniard would rather do a bad job well than a good job poorly, and there is much to suggest this is true. Perhaps this is why it has taken Spain a relatively longer time to develop into an international competitor, even considering the setbacks during Franco's rule.

THE CONCEPT OF INDIVIDUALISM

The Spanish have always asserted their uniqueness. They are determined to succeed by their own initiative and strongly oppose having uninvited ideas imposed on them. What a strange irony, then, that for so many years Spain was controlled and even repressed by outsiders.

In its early history Spain was subject to a good many invasions by Romans, Visigoths, and Moors. Later, during the reign of the Catholic kings, conformity was the key to survival and religious fanaticism the driving force. During the oppressive Franco years, individualism was brutally discouraged, and even severely punished. No wonder that so many liberals, artists, and freethinkers left Spain to pursue their lives elsewhere. When democratic freedom finally came to Spain, its arrival was long overdue.

THE SIESTA

The siesta is one of the best-known aspects of Spanish life—that quiet period in the late afternoon when everything shuts down in Spain, in theory, so that people can go to sleep. The siesta time for stores and businesses is from approximately 2:00 P.M. to 5:00 P.M., while restaurants close from about 4:00 P.M. to 8:00 P.M.

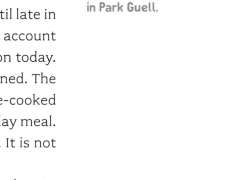

Spanish women taking a siesta on the mosaic seating of the main terrace in Park Guell.

Spain is a hot country, particularly in the mid-afternoon. The traditional reason for the siesta is to enable the workers in the fields to shelter from the heat. They would then be refreshed and able to continue working until late in the evening. People still do work in the fields but this reason does not account for stores and businesses in big cities closing down for the afternoon today. Offices can get hot, too, but most modern buildings are air-conditioned. The main reason for the siesta is that Spaniards like to have a big home-cooked lunch and quite often the whole family will get together for the midday meal. Spaniards also eat later in the evening, and they like to stay up late. It is not unusual to see the streets and bars just starting to fill at midnight.

Today the siesta period is less evident in Madrid or Barcelona than in Granada or Alicante. Big department stores and supermarkets stay open during the siesta, but it is generally noticeable that Spaniards stay away at this time and the people shopping happen to be tourists or foreigners.

URBAN ATTRACTION

Between the last decade of the Franco regime and the first decade of a democratic government, Spain's population steadily migrated to urban areas. Today roughly 77 percent of Spain's population lives in urban areas, compared with 63 percent in 1970. The most populous city is Madrid, followed by Barcelona, Valencia, and Seville. As is the case with most big cities, such as Paris or New York, the inhabitants of Spain's metropolitan areas were often born elsewhere but maintain strong ties to their family home. Migrants from the rural areas to cities (like Madrid and Barcelona) make up a large percentage of the total population of those cities, which are dominated by a growing middle or upper-middle class. Many of these people work in administrative and clerical jobs or in service industries.

The center of life in the city is usually the town center or square. Shopping areas, restaurants, offices, and theaters attract the most people. Traffic is heavy especially during rush hour, but it is common to find traffic congestion on the roads at all hours as Spain's big cities rarely sleep. Parking spaces are few and hard to find, and in some places it is perfectly acceptable to squeeze a car into an illegal spot or to park on a sidewalk.

The Gran Vía is Madrid's main artery. Lined with stores, cinemas, cafés, and restaurants, it bustles with activity day and night.

URBAN HOUSING

Housing has been a big problem in Spain's metropolitan cities since the migration to urban areas began. In the 1960s the government called for a national housing plan, aimed at developing 4 million new dwellings in 15 years. However, the plan focused on large, high-rise, moderately expensive apartment buildings and failed to provide small, modest apartments needed by many.

In 1982 the Socialist government announced a plan to correct the shortage of affordable, decent housing in urban centers, a move that aimed to provide all citizens with their own homes by the 1990s. In 1998 a rehabilitation program was initiated in the historic center of Madrid to address the problem of urban decay and improve housing and infrastructure.

Most middle-class urbanites live in apartment complexes in the cities, or on the cities' outer rims. Outside many towns and cities are planned urbanizations of houses just a few miles away from the town center where the owners may also have a small garden. There are other social implications, such as delayed marriages and more extended family arrangements.

Housing policies now require developers to include low-cost housing in their new projects. The development of more rental housing also helps control rental rates. Property speculation kept housing costs up for many years, but in 2011, after the construction industry bubble burst and the resulting recession, property prices fell by as much as 30 percent and many housing projects have remained unfinished.

THE TRANSFORMATION OF RURAL AREAS

Today 24 percent of Spain's total population lives in the countryside and rural areas. This figure decreases steadily each year as more and more of each new generation move away from the farm to pursue their lives in larger cities. In Spain sons no longer follow their father in traditional occupations and lifestyles. Furthermore the prestige of farming as a way of life is rapidly declining in rural areas.

As Spain opens up to new ideas from the outside world, the traditional rural class becomes exposed to new alternatives in living and working, perhaps alternatives that were never imagined to be possible before. In extreme cases, emigration to larger cities was a matter of life or death. Many farmers were forced to sell their farms when faced with a particularly bad year, and they had to find alternative means of making a living elsewhere.

Tourism has played a role in making some rural villages less isolated. Access has been improved somewhat by the construction of better roads, electricity, and other facilities for the tourist industry. Tourists are attracted to unspoiled areas that provide for skiing, mountain climbing, and hiking in the mountains, or swimming and water sports in coastal villages. In these areas tourism has replaced agriculture as the main source of revenue.

In some Basque villages the traditional social structure has broken down as the value placed on farming has declined. The younger generations are eager to leave home and find jobs in a big city.

EDUCATION

During the Franco years most education was subsidized by the government and administered by the Catholic Church. The system was characteristically traditional, conservative, and authoritarian. At many levels of education, but especially at secondary and university levels, attending school was only an option for the upper classes, making it quite difficult for members of the lower class or those from a rural community to better themselves through education. This contributed to social, cultural, economic, and political differences among the classes.

One of King Juan Carlos's tasks when he came to power was educational reform, and it has been a major issue for the Socialist government ever since. The stated purposes of the country's educational system are social and cultural integration to build a unified nation, economic integration to create opportunities for all, and political integration to maintain democratic values.

Since 1991, when the General Regulation of the Educational System Act came into force, primary (for ages 6 to 11) and secondary (12 to 16) education has been free and compulsory. On successfully completing the secondary stage of education, pupils are awarded the certificate of Secondary Education Graduate, which gives access to the *Bachillerarato* (bah-CHEE-yay-re-RAH-toh) and medium-grade training cycles in Spanish schools. This post-compulsory secondary education lasts two years and is for students who are 16 to 18 years old. University or higher education is optional, but entrance examinations are compulsory if one chooses to attend.

Spain is now experiencing a zeal for education at a level never observed before. As a result of the government's educational reforms, nearly all children between the ages of 6 and 16 are enrolled in either a primary or secondary school. Although all schools are required by law to provide religious instruction, this is voluntary for pupils.

Children in a group photo at a school in Barcelona.

UNIVERSITY The university system in Spain has undergone many changes. In 1983 the Socialist government sought to lessen the central government's control over the universities and their curriculum and gave each public university increased autonomy.

Students can choose a four- to six-year university program that offers liberal and professional studies, such as law, medicine, sciences, and humanities. Alternatively they can enroll in a technical college that offers degrees in engineering, architecture, and other applied skills after three years of study.

In 2002 public expenditure on educational institutions absorbed 4.5 percent of the country's GDP. Surveys conducted in 2011 indicated there were more than 1.5 million students in Spain's universities. More students are enrolling in the professional and liberal study programs, seeking careers in medicine, law, and other professions. At present there are 75 universities in Spain, 50 of which are public and 25 are private. Of the private universities, seven belong to the Catholic Church. There is also an Open University based in Madrid that teaches by mail, radio, and television.

The Menéndez Pelayo International University building in Santander.

CHANGES IN ATTITUDES

During the 36 years of Franco's authoritarian and conservative rule, Spain was isolated from the rest of the world and essentially locked in its own past. This also meant it lagged behind its Western European neighbors in social and cultural development. With the introduction of democracy, freedom of expression and social and political changes have contributed substantially to creating new opportunities and lifestyles for Spaniards.

Although once the most conservative country in Western Europe, Spain is becoming increasingly liberal. Freedom of the press and the outlawing of censorship have spawned a host of newspapers, magazines, and literature reflecting the changes in social and political mores all over the world. After being exposed to such contemporary perspectives, Spaniards have adopted some of these progressive views and changed their way of life. This is especially so with the younger generation: socialist sentiments are popular among university students, and public displays of affection are common.

Divorce was not legal during the Franco regime because the Catholic Church opposed it and the conservative government all but condemned it. The only way for a couple to end their marriage was by legal separation or annulment, both almost impossible to obtain. In the 1980s, however, 80 percent of Spanish people polled said they were not opposed to divorce and more than half were not opposed to the use of contraception. Divorce rates have soared since the new legislation known as the express divorce bill was introduced by the Socialist government in 2005. The National Institute of Statistics states that 126,952 divorces were registered in 2006, a 74.3 percent increase on the previous year.

Youths enjoying a bowling game in Barcelona. The young today have more freedom to pursue their own interests.

TODAY'S YOUTH

Young Spaniards of all classes are becoming avid consumers, spending most of their money on clothes, music, motor scooters, and evenings out at clubs. This consumerism reflects the reduction in class differences among the young people, as distinctions by material possessions become increasingly less obvious. In addition they are knowledgeable and enthusiastic about American trends in music, fashion, and movies.

THE CHANGING ROLE OF WOMEN

The role of women is changing in Spain as new opportunities and freedoms arise. The country's dramatic industrialization programs have encouraged women to join the labor force. In 1940 women represented less than 15 percent of the working population. In 2004 that figure had reached 47.7 percent. As a result there are more child-care centers and more liberal attitudes about the place of women in society, whether politically or legally.

Modern Spanish women chatting in the streets.

Although poorer women have always had to work for a living, usually as domestics, they are now seeking more jobs in the service sector as salespeople and waitresses. Middle-class women are picking up jobs in technical fields as pharmacists, clerks, and teachers. They generally work part-time and are paid less than their male counterparts for the same position. Many working women, however, are not willing to give up the responsibility of their home or family life. It is not unusual for them to divide their time more or less equally among their homes, children, and jobs, unwilling to relinquish any bit of their newfound freedom or their long-held traditions.

More women are also assuming roles once reserved for men, entering male-dominated fields such as politics, engineering, architecture, law, medicine, chemistry, and the social sciences. Women also work in libraries, museums, banks, publishing, health care, and marketing, and as police officers in the big cities.

Better career options are available across all age groups. Young girls join the workforce as soon as they are able, working after school in offices and stores in order to contribute to the family income and have enough money for their own clothes, makeup, movies, and other pastimes. For the first time in recent history many middle-class women are opting to finish their education, returning to school after their children have left home.

Women have made significant progress in legal matters as well. During the more conservative years women had almost no legal rights. They could not sign a legal document or receive a salary without first seeking their husbands' permission. In addition a married woman had no right to an inheritance and was liable to be punished severely for adultery, while the man could count on escaping punishment altogether.

Craftswomen gainfully employed in the exquisite art of lace-making.

INTERNET LINKS

http://gospain.about.com/

This informative website is also a travel guide that provides detailed information on the lifestyle, cultures, and peoples of Spain.

http://spanishschoolsinspain.com/

This is an exhaustive resource about schools and the educational system in Spain.

www.newadvent.org/cathen/03769a.htm

This website provides information on the great popular hero of the chivalrous age of Spain, El Cid. The exploits of El Cid are the subject of the epic poem of the same name.

RELIGION

The famous Cathedral of Santiago de Compostela in the capital of Galicia. The cathedral is the reputed burial place of Saint James the Greater, one of the apostles of Jesus Christ. It is the destination of the Way of Saint James, a major historical pilgrimage route since the Middle Ages.

8

ROMAN CATHOLICISM IS THE major religion of Spain. The Center for Sociological Investigation (CIS), an independent government agency, conducts surveys on trends and opinions. In 2012 a CIS survey reported that 71 percent of respondents in Spain consider themselves Roman Catholic.

Other Christian groups make up less than 10 percent of the total population and include Eastern Orthodox, Protestant and evangelical denominations, Christian Scientists, Jehovah's Witnesses, Seventh-day Adventists, and members of The Church of Jesus Christ of Latter-day

The constitution provides for freedom of religion in Spain and there is no official state religion. The law prohibits the collection of census data based on religious belief, which limits the ability to compile statistical data on religions practiced in Spain.

Inside the Mezquita at Córdoba. The Mezquita began as a mosque built on the site of a Visigothic church, some ornate details of which were preserved. In the 16th century, King Charles V built a baroque cathedral in the center of the Mezquita.

Saints (Mormons). Less than 10 percent of the total population follows Islam, Judaism, Buddhism, Hinduism, and the Bahai Faith. The Federation of Jewish Communities estimates that there are 48,000 Jews in Spain.

ROMAN AND MEDIEVAL SPAIN

A predominantly urban religion, Christianity spread through Roman Hispania during the second and third centuries. Hispania was the Roman name for the Iberian Peninsula. Large areas of the countryside remained untouched for many decades, as did most of Cantabria and the Basque region. By the beginning of the fourth century, Hispania had a Christian minority and after the official recognition of the church in the early fourth century, the following increased greatly until almost the entire peninsula had become Christian. In A.D. 711 Muslim forces invaded and conquered the Iberian Peninsula. Islamic Spain (711—1492) was a multicultural mix of the people of three monotheistic religions: Muslims, Christians, and Jews. Although the Christians and Jews lived with certain restrictions, the three groups managed to get along together and to benefit from the presence of each other.

During the Middle Ages, when Spain was a collection of kingdoms, religion was the unifying force that held the kingdoms together. This unity persisted over centuries of crusading along the Iberian Peninsula and culminated in the reign of the Catholic kings, Isabella and Ferdinand, who had complete control over both religion and government.

THE INQUISITION AND THE FRANCO YEARS

The Catholic kings sought to purge the peninsula of other religious groups by means of a cruel, relentless crusade called the Spanish Inquisition. In the end the Spanish Inquisition outlived its strongest defenders, Isabella and Ferdinand, by over 300 years.

Catholicism was officially declared the state religion in 1851 by a pact between the Vatican and the Spanish government. In 1931 the religion was renounced by the Republic. The Franco years restored the privileges of the Catholic Church, making Catholicism the only religion to have legal status. No

Protestant church, Jewish synagogue, or Muslim mosque was allowed to advertise services, identify its religious beliefs, own property, or publish literature, and mobs made countless attacks on differing places of worship. Franco had the power to appoint clergy, and his government directly subsidized the Church, paid priests' salaries, and reconstructed numerous church buildings that had been damaged in the Civil War. Franco passed laws abolishing divorce and the use of contraceptives, and religious instruction was made mandatory in all schools. Countless artists, liberals, and intellectuals left Spain during these years to escape Franco's repressive church-state.

CATHOLICISM IN PRESENT-DAY SPAIN

King Juan Carlos I did much to lessen the importance of the Catholic Church in the everyday life of Spain. Catholicism is no longer the official religion, but the Church still enjoyed a privileged status until recently. Churches and Catholic schools received financial support from the government until the late 1980s, despite protests from Socialist officials and party members.

The ornate interior of the Santa Maria de Montserrat Benedictine abbey in Catalonia. During Franco's rule, it served as a place of refuge for the many wanted men.

In addition to government-imposed changes, there are many other forces transforming the relationship between the Catholic Church and the people of Spain. The economic and demographic shift from a rural society to an urban one has contributed significantly to secularization. Traditionally rural villages and small towns celebrated and glorified the local church and clergy, and villagers found great satisfaction in religious traditions. But as Spaniards embrace industrialization and capitalism, urban culture and mass media are replacing the Church in social influence.

THE SPANISH INQUISITION

The Inquisition did not begin in Spain, but it did gain the most notoriety there. Instituted in 1480, the Spanish Inquisition was a separate tribunal of the Roman Catholic Church designed to rid the country of heretics, people who opposed the teachings of the Church. Set up by Ferdinand and Isabella, the primary tenets of the Spanish Inquisition were:

- *to offer protection to converted Jews,* conversos, *from retaliation by hostile members of the Jewish faith and to make sure they did not return to Judaism;*
- *to seek out false converts, called* marranos, *Jews who continued to practice their faith in private;*
- *to prevent the relapse of converted Moors, called* moriscos, *and their alliance with heretical groups.*

Shortly after it began, however, the Spanish Inquisition was accused of numerous abuses. Accusations of heresy ran rampant, and innocent, faithful people were unjustly punished by public trial and condemnation. This usually took the form of torture, strangulation, or burning at the stake, and members of some Christian groups were sentenced to life in prison. More than 13,000 conversos were put on trial during the first 12 years of the Spanish Inquisition. To eliminate ties between the Jewish community and conversos, the Jews of Spain were expelled in 1492. Muslims were also expelled or forced into Catholic conversion. It has been estimated that 31,912 heretics were burned at the stake. The Spanish Inquisition was not abolished in Spain until 1808, during the brief reign of Joseph Bonaparte.

OBSERVANCE OF CATHOLICISM

With higher living standards, most Spaniards now identify themselves by material means more than by religious beliefs. It is generally accepted in Spain that to be a good Catholic is no longer synonymous with being a successful person and that to be a priest or clergy member is no longer a source of intense family pride as it was in the past. As a sign of the times, the number of ordained priests in Spain has been declining since the 1980s.

Roman Catholics in Spain today pay more attention to the observance of rites and celebrations than to regular attendance at Mass. Few Spaniards attend Mass on a regular basis, but many believe in the teachings of the faith. Seven sacraments, or rites of the Roman Catholic Church, mark the observance of the religion.

BAPTISM is spiritual birth; it cleanses a person of "original sin," a state in which Roman Catholics believe people are born deprived of grace as a result of Adam and Eve's disobedience to God in the garden of Eden.

A priest conducting mass at a cathedral in Spain.

Catholic parents usually have their babies baptized soon after birth. Parents choose the baby's godparents, who will remain closely involved with the child throughout his or her life.

Those at the ceremony, usually the parents, godparents, and other family members, dress formally. The baby is dressed in a white robe, which in Spain may have been passed down from generation to generation. Spaniards give a newly baptized baby gifts in the form of jewelry.

RECONCILIATION is the sacrament by which a person confesses his or her sins to a priest and receives God's forgiveness. Sins range from telling a small lie to serious offenses such as adultery.

The confessor makes an act of contrition—sincere remorse for having sinned and resolution not to sin again—and shows repentance by saying prayers or doing works of mercy. The priest grants absolution to the confessor, who is thus forgiven and reconciled to the Church.

Roman Catholics who have reached the age of reason are encouraged to make their confession frequently, especially during Lent, the season before Easter.

HOLY COMMUNION commemorates Christ's Last Supper. Catholics receive a wafer and wine, which they believe become Christ's body and blood at Mass.

THE LEGACY OF THE CHURCH

There are countless reminders of the glory that was the Roman Catholic Church at its most powerful in Spain. The country boasts outstanding cathedrals in more than 40 of its cities; Seville has the biggest and tallest cathedral in Spain and the largest Gothic building in the world, but the most impressive religious building in Spain is the Mezquita at Córdoba.

The legacy of the church in Spain is also evident in everyday life. Spaniards are often named after religious figures such as the Virgin Mary. Many girls have María as a first name (for example, María Luisa or María Eugenia), while José and Jesús are popular boys' names.

Cities and occupations often have a patron saint as their protector. Spaniards also say prayers or make offerings to patron saints in special circumstances, such as sickness, a serious accident, or a difficult problem.

Spanish homes are often decorated with images of saints, and many Spaniards wear a crucifix and religious medals around the neck.

Santiago de Compostela, in Galicia, considered by Catholics the third holiest city in the world (after Rome and Jerusalem), is the focus of Spain's most important pilgrimage. In 2009 a total of 145,877 people made the pilgrimage to Santiago de Compostela by car, bus, train, plane, bicycle, donkey, or on foot.

Spaniards make their first Holy Communion between the ages of 6 and 10 years and these are quite important social events. Girls wear white gowns, with a veil or floral hair band, and boys wear charming outfits, such as sailor suits.

CONFIRMATION is a renewal of a person's baptismal promises; it admits the person to full membership in the Roman Catholic Church and solidifies his or her faith. Catholics in Spain, as elsewhere, are usually confirmed between the ages of 12 and 18 years.

HOLY MATRIMONY bonds the bride and groom as one for life. Divorce is not acknowledged in the Roman Catholic Church, although it is legal in Spain.

It is common for the young Spanish bride to keep her white gown, a symbol of her purity. In some small towns of the Pyrenees it is customary to dress up the village statue of the Virgin with one of the wedding dresses of the newlyweds of the area.

HOLY ORDERS is the sacrament of ordination, which admits a baptized man to the priesthood. Roman Catholic priests take the vow of celibacy and never marry, in order to commit totally to leading and serving the community. In Spain priests are called *Padre* (PAH-dray), or "Father."

EXTREME UNCTION is the last sacrament in the life of a Roman Catholic. Also known as last rites or the anointing of the sick, it is administered when death is imminent, absolving the recipient of his or her sins and preparing him or her to meet God.

A priest performs extreme unction by anointing a sick person's forehead with consecrated olive oil and praying over him or her.

INTERNET LINKS

www.state.gov/j/drl/rls/irf/2005/51582.htm

This site provides information on many aspects of religion, societal attitudes to religion, and the status of religious freedom in Spain.

www.bbc.co.uk/religion/religions/islam/history/spain_1.shtml

This website contains information on Islamic Spain (711—1492), with links to information on Spain's Islamic legacy and the architecture of Muslim Spain.

www.jewishvirtuallibrary.org/jsource/History/Inquisition.html

This site provides information on the Spanish Inquisition, a Roman Catholic tribunal for discovery and punishment of heresy.

LANGUAGE

A poster announces details of a bullfight in Castilian. In Spain, Castilian Spanish is the official language. Catalan is widely spoken in the northeast, Galician in the northwest, and Basque in the north.

9

SPANISH IS A ROMANCE language—based on Latin—which was spread by the Roman conquerors when Rome held power over most of the Western world. It began as a regional dialect of Latin, and through widespread usage became a formal language with grammatical rules and a literature of its own.

What the rest of the world knows as Spanish is called "Castilian" in Spain, because it was originally the dialect of the kingdom of Castile.

There are three co-official languages in Spain: Euskera (Basque), Galego (Galician), and Català (Catalan). The official language of Spain is Castilian, which is the language generally perceived to be "Spanish." Castilian Spanish is also the official language in many South American countries, including Argentina, Chile, Colombia, Mexico, Ecuador, and Uruguay.

A woman sitting in a newspaper stand in Granada.

Castilian is the official language of Spain and all Spanish government business. Castilian is spoken mostly in central Spain.

Around 74 percent of the Spanish population speaks Castilian Spanish regularly, but one in four Spaniards speaks a language other than Castilian. There are three important regional languages in Spain, each with its own structure, vocabulary, and literature: Catalan, Galician, and Basque. About 17 percent of Spaniards speak Catalan, while 7 percent speak Galician, and 2 percent speak Basque. All regional language speakers can and do also speak Castilian. In addition to these three regional languages, there are important dialects spoken throughout the country, such as those in Valencia and Aragón.

An organization called the Real Academia de la Lengua Española (Royal Academy of the Spanish Language) acts as the governing body of the Spanish language. It determines accepted spellings of words, ruling whether new words can be considered proper Spanish or not. Of course people will use whatever words they want, official or not. It also produces the dictionary that is the ultimate linguistic authority in Spain and Latin America.

The interior of a Spanish bookstore in Costa del Sol. During the Franco years, regional language books and classics were destroyed.

REGIONAL LANGUAGES

The language differences in Spain make for a frustrating time when one is traveling from one region to another. Road signs are sometimes in the language of the region, making it hard for travelers to understand if they are not familiar with the particular tongue. More important than that, however, is the fact that these language differences often create divisions among the people. The country has been threatened on numerous occasions with partial division by related independence movements, most notably by the Basques.

During Spain's long history, many governments were not always tolerant of the language differences. Successive rulers equated sameness of tongue with stability in government, and as a result the regional dialects were frequently outlawed. Francisco Franco in particular held rigid views on the subject. Under his regime regional languages that had been permitted during the Second Republic were restricted in favor of Castilian. Many literary classics and school books, if not written in Castilian, were burned. The publication of regional language newspapers was prohibited, and the use of regional languages was banned from public offices.

It was not until the 1960s that the government became more tolerant. In Spain today respect for all regional languages is encouraged. Many schools now teach regional languages and their respective literature as part of the curriculum.

Girls doing their work in a school in Andalusia.

CATALAN Catalan is spoken in the region of Catalonia in northeastern Spain. Closely related to the Provençal language of southern France, Catalan is said to be closer to French in vocabulary and accent than to Castilian Spanish.

One of the Romance languages, Catalan is derived from the rich languages of the Oc linguistic region in France. More literature has been written in Catalan than in either Galician or Basque.

There are subtypes of the Catalan language, such as Valencian spoken in Valencia and Balearic in the Balearic Islands. A highly localized dialect called *Chapurriao* (chah-poo-ree-ow) is spoken in Aragón.

GALICIAN Galician is spoken in Galicia, on the northwestern coast of Spain. Galicia borders Portugal and the regional language is closely related to Portuguese and was probably a Portuguese dialect spoken in this Spanish territory. Galician also has its roots in the Romance languages. It is primarily a rural language and is thus not heard much in the larger cities of the region.

Galician nationalists tend to feel that Galician should be given precedence over Castilian in schools, public offices, and business transactions.

BASQUE Of all the languages in the world, and certainly among those native to Spain, Basque—called *Euskera* (yoo-SKAY-rah) in Basque—is spoken in the Basque provinces and stands out in particular for its unique linguistic characteristics.

Although it is popularly thought to be spoken throughout the western and central Pyrenees regions in ancient times, Basque is now limited in Spain to the province of Guipúcoza, parts of Vizcaya and Navarra, and a corner of Álava.

Perhaps no other language has given so much trouble to linguistic scholars and philologists, as no one can trace the true origins of Basque. It is possibly related to no other language except that of a small area in the Caucasus Mountains of the former Soviet Union. The Basque characteristic of compounding words carries echoes of prehistory. For instance, the Basque names for some weapons and tools contain the word for "stone" as part of their root meaning. The word for "knife" translates as "stone-that-cuts," a spear is a "stone-stick," and the word for "ceiling" means literally "roof-of-the-cave."

It is said that the Basque language can only be learned at "mother's knee." In fact its extremely difficult vocabulary and grammatical structure have elicited a Spanish proverb: "When God wanted to punish the Devil, he condemned him for seven years to study Basque." In 1978 Basque and Castilian Spanish became the official languages of the autonomous Basque country of Spain.

Arabic inscriptions adorn the Nasrid Palace of the Calat Alhambra in Granada.

ARABIC INFLUENCE ON SPANISH

The Moors occupied Spain for 750 years, so it is no wonder that at least 4,000 Arabic words and Arabic-derived phrases have been absorbed into the Spanish language.

Traditional Spanish names reflect the importance of the family. Spanish women customarily retain their maiden name after marriage. For instance, if Eva Peña marries Emilio Martínez, she becomes Señora Eva Peña de Martínez. The de *("day") means, in a literal sense, that Eva is "of" her husband.*

Eva and Emilio's children's last names would be Martínez Peña. In the next generation, the mother's maiden name is dropped, unless it is a famous one. In correspondence, both last names (Señor Martínez Peña) are used, but in conversation, only the first last name (Señor Martínez) is used.

Spaniards consider the first last name the more important one: Martínez Peña would be alphabetized under "M" rather than "P." The concept of a middle name does not exist in Spain, where people might have one or many first names and two last names.

It is also customary to name the firstborn son after the father. For instance Emilio Martínez's son would also be called Emilio Martínez, although in conversation, especially with close relatives and friends, the son's name would include a diminutive—Emilito, which means "little Emilio." The practice is also extended to female children, although it is not as common. If Eva had a daughter named Eva, she would be called Evita by family and friends. Ita *(EE-tah) is a suffix for "little one."*

Words beginning with "al," for instance, come from Arabic: *alabastro* (a-la-BAS-tro) means "alabaster"; *alejar* (al-lay-har) means "to distance" or "repel". Because the Moors were well advanced in the study of medicine, science, and astronomy, they left a legacy of such terms, many of which have traveled to other languages, including English and French, through Spanish. Some obvious examples are words like *algebra*, *alcohol*, *chemistry*, *nadir*, *zenith*, *alkaline*, and *cipher*. Interestingly even words like *checkmate*, *influenza*, *typhoon*, *orange*, and *cable* can be traced back to Arabic origins.

A common expression in Spain, *¡Ojalá!* (o-ha-LAH), meaning "I hope that" or "so it may come to pass," probably comes from the Muslim war cry *Wa Allah* (WAH AHL-lah). The expression *si Dios quiere* (see dee-AWS kee-AY-reh), which means "God willing" or "if God wants to," is similar to the common Arabic expression *Insha Allah* (EN-shah AHL-lah).

There is one very unusual and interesting characteristic of the Castilian language and those who speak it. In central Spain, and a few points north, a distinct lisp ("th" sound) is pronounced with the letters s, c (soft c when followed by e or i), and z. For instance, Gracias, which means "thank you", is pronounced "GRAH-thee-uhs," and Saragossa, Aragón's capital, is pronounced "Thar-ah-go-tha." In all other areas of Spain, the soft c and z are pronounced as s. It is interesting to note that as Castilian is generally thought of as "high Spanish," the most prestigious form, the lisp is often practiced in areas where it generally would not apply.

There are many theories as to how and why the Castilian "lisp" came into being. The most frequent explanation is that a certain Castilian king spoke with a lisp, and his courtiers, in their obsessive desire to be like the king, imitated and later popularized it. This story has become an urban legend, it is unlikely to be based on fact. Another theory is that the lisp developed from the language of the early Greek settlers in Spain (modern Greek retains the lisp for certain letters). Still another theory maintains that the lisp developed from Arabic speech and found its way into the Spanish language during the Moors' 750-year dominance.

The Moors also lent their language to the names of many cities and towns. Generally all those that begin with "al" were designated by the Moors during their occupation; for example, Almería, Albarracín, and Alicante.

NONVERBAL FORMS OF COMMUNICATION

Spaniards, being an expressive people, use gestures with or to substitute for spoken words. However, it would be considered rude for an outsider to imitate their mannerisms.

Certain obviously insulting gestures, generally understood as rude and offensive in most other countries as well, are also used in Spain. Flicking the teeth with the thumbnail in the direction of the second party, wiggling fingers from the nose, and grabbing the left arm with the right while making a left-handed fist are all thought to be offensive and are commonly avoided except in the most provocative of situations.

Tapping the left elbow with the right hand is a sign that someone is a penny-pincher. Pulling down the lower eyelid while someone is talking means that the listener doubts what the speaker is saying.

Making a repeated clicking noise by holding the thumb and second finger together and snapping the wrist rapidly indicates excitement or strong appreciation.

Holding up both the little and index fingers with the knuckles facing outward and holding this up in front of a man signals that his wife or girlfriend is being unfaithful.

Spaniards are quick to show affection, and it is perfectly natural for men and women to embrace when meeting. They also tend to stand close to one another when talking.

However, the same rules of familiarity do not apply between strangers. Eye contact between a man and a woman who are not introduced can carry a meaning of romantic interest. A woman who returns a man's gaze is interpreted as indicating that she is available. Similarly it is common for men to express their admiration for a woman on the street by whistling or calling out. They are said to mean no harm, and the women generally do not acknowledge them.

In all it is natural for Spaniards to express themselves passionately in their daily communication, and visitors to Spain will likely find every conversation a lively and animated exchange.

INTERNET LINKS

www.omniglot.com/writing/basque.htm

This is an online encyclopedia dedicated to the written and spoken Basque (Euskera) language, including the history of the language.

www.rae.es/rae.html

This is the website of the Royal Academy of the Spanish language, with links to a very useful and extensive online Spanish language dictionary.

Although differences in lifestyle and cultural traditions still exist, the process of assimilation of the Spanish population has gone on for such a long time that identification of Spain's ethnic groups will soon be based only on language.

ARTS

The City of Arts and Sciences in Valencia is one of the most important cultural centers of modern Spain.

10

THE SPANISH ARE AN artistic people, who place great value on creativity and self-expression. Each province of Spain has a cultural institution, overseen by the Ministry of Culture.

Spain's cultural center is Madrid, although Barcelona, Valencia, Bilbao, and other large urban centers actively patronize the arts as well. Madrid hosts big arts festivals and offers other cultural attractions throughout the year. The massive Auditorio Nacional de Música is the capital's most important concert hall for classical music; the Teatro Real offers classical concerts, opera, and other forms of entertainment; and the Teatro de la Zarzuela is famous for its ever-changing program of ballet, concerts, opera, and a form of traditional Spanish operetta known as *zarzuela* (zar-zoo-EH-lah).

The Teatro Real, or Royal Theater, is a major opera house in Madrid.

The interior of Sagrada Família. Designed by Catalan architect Antoni Gaudí, the cathedral was listed as a World Heritage Site by UNESCO in 2010.

The Museo Nacional Centro de Arte Reina Sofía (Queen Sofia Art Center), a museum of contemporary art, is one of the most vital centers for contemporary art worldwide. It hosts Spain's international contemporary art fair, ARCO, which attracts the world's top dealers.

The most famous museum in Madrid is the Museo Nacional del Prado, one of the greatest museums in the world. The Prado is home to extraordinary collections by artists such as Domenikos Theotokopoulos, known as El Greco, and Francisco Goya y Lucientes.

Barcelona is not without its own cultural attractions, most of which are music-oriented since Catalans are widely known to be music lovers. The Gran Teatro del Liceu is respected as one of the world's greatest opera houses. Every year the Sónar Festival draws crowds of musicians, artists, and spectators. The Sónar combines music and multimedia art in experimental ways. Barcelona is also famous worldwide for Modernista architecture, specifically the work of Antoni Gaudí.

The City of Arts and Sciences in Valencia is a unique complex devoted to scientific and cultural dissemination. It is made up of five main elements. The Hemisfèric (IMAX cinema and digital projections) was opened in 1998. The Umbracle is a landscaped vantage point and car park. The Príncipe Felipe Science Museum was designed by Valencian architect Santiago Calatrava. The Oceanográfico opened in 2001 and is the largest aquarium in Europe with more than 500 marine species. The Palau de les Arts Reina Sofía is a multi-hall auditorium that opened in 2005. The Ágora gives the complex a multifunctional space.

EARLY MASTERS

Spain's Golden Age in art, architecture, literature, and music spanned the 16th and early part of the 17th century.

PAINTING Among the great artists, the leading figures were Francisco de Zurbarán (1598—1664), Diego Rodríguez de Silva y Velázquez (1599—1660), Bartolomé Esteban Murillo (1617—82), and Domenikos Theotokopoulos (1541—1614), a Greek from the island of Crete who settled in Toledo when he was in his 30s and spent the rest of his life there. El Greco, as Theotokopoulos was and still is called in Spain, typified Spain's Golden Age artists like no other, even though he was not a native Spaniard. He is known for his haunting images of biblical and religious themes and his striking paintings of Toledo.

A statue of Velázquez sits in front of the Prado Museum in Madrid.

For hundreds of years, the most highly regarded of all Spanish painters was Diego Rodríguez de Silva y Velázquez. He was born into a well-to-do family from Seville, and his early years were filled with art lessons. He became a court painter for King Philip IV in 1623. One of Velázquez's greatest works is a portrait of Pope Innocent X, painted in 1650. Toward the end of his life, the artist painted his masterpiece, *Las Meninas* (*The Ladies-in-Waiting*), an example of technical perfection for future generations of artists.

Murillo, like Velázquez, was born in Seville. He had virtually no formal training but exhibited a lot of innate talent. He was revered in his day for his religious paintings, most notably of the Immaculate Conception, and his paintings of street urchins and peasants. Another of Spain's great artists, Francisco de Zurbarán, was born in Extremadura in 1598. The region's treeless plains and sunbaked landscapes are mirrored in his powerful and austere paintings. His most renowned works, a series of religious paintings, are installed at the Monastery of Guadelupe in Extremadura. The only recorded woman painter of this period was Josefa D'Obidos (1630—84). Born in Seville, she lived most of her life in Portugal and excelled in still-life painting.

Although Francisco Goya y Lucientes (1746—1828) came after the Golden Age, his paintings and etchings are among the best in the world. He was a court painter during Charles IV's reign, and his later works dealt largely with themes of violence, political uprisings, religious allegories, and supernatural beings.

Many of Goya's paintings, such as *The Witches' Sabbath*, had a nightmarish quality, and his pair of *Maja* (ma-ha) paintings—one of a clothed woman, the other of her naked—caused a stir. The artist's unique personal vision and artistic brilliance made him one of the most important social commentators of his time. His etchings and drawings of bullfights called the *Tauromaquia* were published in 1816. In the *Black Paintings*, executed on the walls of his house between 1819 and 1824, Goya gave expression to his darkest visions. A similar nightmarish quality haunts the satirical *Disparates*, a series of etchings also called *Proverbios*.

ARCHITECTURE The greatest architects of the Golden Age were Juan de Herrera (1530—97) and José Churriguera (1665—1725). Herrera was the principal architect of King Philip II's massive, granite palace-monastery, and his works came to typify Spanish Renaissance style.

Construction of El Escorial, as the palace is called, began in 1563 and was completed in 1584. It made a great impression in its day but is no longer considered an architectural masterpiece because of its austerity and gloom. Nevertheless the building is one of the most visited in Spain. Aside from being the home of Philip II, El Escorial contains a beautiful library with more than 40,000 rare manuscripts and ancient books, including the diaries of Saint Theresa of Ávila.

The museum on the property houses works by great masters such as Velázquez, El Greco, Tintoretto, and Rubens, while the church contains priceless frescoes. But perhaps the most fascinating feature of El Escorial is the Royal Pantheon, which contains the tomb of almost every Spanish king since Charles I.

The architectural works of Churriguera are much more elaborate than those of his predecessor Herrera. The best example of his Spanish baroque style is the main altar of San Esteban in Salamanca outside of Madrid.

LITERATURE The greatest literary figures of Spain's Golden Age were novelist Miguel de Cervantes y Saavedra (1547—1616) and dramatists Félix Lope de Vega y Carpio (1562—1635) and Pedro Calderón de la Barca (1600—81). Cervantes, the author of the immortal, world-famous *Don Quixote*, was born in Alcalá de Henares, east of Madrid, and his house is now a museum. In writing *Don Quixote*, the tale about an idealist and dreamer knight whose madness led him to "right all wrongs," Cervantes not only created a glorious work of fiction, but a national hero as well. Don Quixote has come to symbolize the heroic pattern of Spanish life and honor, as a man who committed his whole being to upholding justice without regard to danger. In keeping with the Spanish character, human dignity and innate goodness are believed to ultimately lead one to immortality.

The ceiling of the library at El Escorial, built by King Philip II.

Lope was a lyrical genius whose great body of work revolutionized theater in his day and for centuries to come. Cervantes himself said the man was a "prodigy of nature." Lope was a devout Catholic, and many of his plays had a religious theme. *Peribáñez and the Comendador of Ocaña* and *Fuente Ovejuna* are two of his best and most renowned plays. Lope took great inspiration from *The Celestina*, a story of love, lust, and moral retribution written in 1499 by Fernando de Rojas, himself a Jewish convert to Catholicism.

Calderón is best known for his works *The Mayor of Zalamea* and *Life Is a Dream*. His plays have a religious and philosophical theme, and like Lope, Calderón spent his later years as a priest.

The greatest poet of the Golden Age was Luis de Góngora y Argote (1561—1627), who gave his name to the poetic style called *gongorismo* (GON-go-REES-moh), an embellished, wordy, fantastical style of verse. Góngora's most celebrated piece of work is *Solitudes*, written in 1613.

MUSIC The regional diversity of Spain is strongly reflected in its music. Spain has produced many important composers, the art form of musical composition having flourished during the reign of Isabella and Ferdinand. Juan del Encina was a playwright, poet, and composer of secular vocal music and a favorite of Prince Juan, the only son of the Catholic kings. Antonio de Cabezón (1510—66), called the Spanish Bach, was an important composer for the keyboard and clavichord, and Cristóbal de Morales (circa 1500—53) for his church music. Tomás Luis de Victoria (1549—1611), a master of vocal melodies, is most famous for his Requiem Mass "Officium defunctorum," written in 1605 for the Empress Maria. Perhaps the most significant record of Spanish folk music is found in the *Cancionero de Palacio* (*Palace Song Book*), a collection of 500 or more varied musical compositions from the 15th and 16th centuries. Of these 75 were written by Juan del Encina.

SPANISH NATIONALIST COMPOSERS

In the early 1800s Italian singers and composers dominated the lyric theaters of Spain. The nationalist movement was a reaction against this overwhelming presence. Felipe Pedrell (1841—1922) resurrected the works of great Spanish composers that had long been forgotten. He was a key figure in improving the quality of Spanish church music and, as Lionel Salter wrote in *Spain: a Nation in Turbulence*, condemned the "showy Italiante styles that secularized and theatricalized religious music." He stressed the importance of writing music rooted in Spanish culture. This philosophy guided and influenced his three famous students: Isaac Albéniz, Enrique Granados, and Manuel de Falla. Albéniz (1860—1909) is best known for his piano works, many of which have since been arranged by others for guitar. Albéniz's *Suite Iberia*, originally a piano work consisting of 12 movements, uses traditional dance rhythms including the jota, polo, and fandango along with imitations of flamenco guitars, gypsy music, and church bells. Among the best-known works of Granados (1867—1916) are the *12 Danzas Españolas* (*12 Spanish Dances*) and *Valses Poéticos* (*Poetic Waltzes*). Manuel de Falla (1876—1946) began formal piano lessons in 1885. He wrote stage, orchestral, choral, and chamber works as well as works for solo instruments.

20TH-CENTURY MASTERS

After Spain's Golden Age, artistic achievement in the 18th and 19th centuries was considered to lack vitality and imagination. The 20th century, however, broke new ground, especially in the area of architecture. Antoni Gaudí (1852—1926) was one of the most imaginative architects the world has ever seen. His style was decorative and ornate, bordering on the fantastical, and he endowed his native Barcelona with many of his works.

The most impressive of these is the Temple expiatori de la Sagrada Familia (the Expiatory Church of the Holy Family), begun in 1882 and still

Casa Amatller (*left*) and Casa Batlló (*right*) are part of Barcelona's famous Illa de la Discòrdia (Block of Discord), which features a range of unique modernist buildings.

not completed, mostly because modern-day architects do not understand Gaudí's plans. It has always been an expiatory church, which means that since the outset it has been built from donations. Tragically Gaudí was killed by a streetcar. His funeral procession was as elaborate as any great leader's, testimony to his popularity in his beloved country. His body is buried in the crypt of the Sagrada Familia.

Spanish artists greatly influenced 20th-century art movements. Perhaps no one was more influential than Pablo Picasso (1881—1973), the most productive artist of his century.

Born in Málaga, Picasso emigrated to France. He was one of the founders of Cubism, an artistic movement concerned with abstract and geometric representation of forms.

Picasso's personal vision revolutionized all forms of art, from sculpture and pottery to drawing and painting. One of his most famous works is *Guernica* (1937), a huge painting depicting the horrors of the Spanish Civil War, specifically the bombing of the Basque town of Guernica by Italian and Nazi fascists. Picasso refused to let the painting enter Spain while Franco was still alive. Today it hangs in the Centro de Arte Reina Sofia in Madrid.

Other important painters include Juan Gris (1887—1927), also a Cubist who emigrated to France; Joan Miró (1893—1983), a Barcelona native known for his bold, expressive surrealist images; and Salvador Dalí (1904—89), a Surrealist who, like Picasso and Gris, spent much of his creative life outside of Spain.

Dalí's art deserves special mention because of its fantastical subject matter: images and emotions of the artist's productive subconscious. Dalí was a great friend and sometime collaborator of Spanish filmmaker Luis Buñuel (1900—83), who spent much of his life in Mexico. Buñuel's unique, creative approach to filmmaking influenced many.

Changes in expression at the beginning of the 20th century were also reflected in literary works from that era. A group of brilliant writers and poets, who called themselves the "Generation of 1898," produced some of the finest literature in Spain. The "Generation of 1898" was the embodiment of new feelings developing, especially among the intellectuals, toward the emerging Spanish nation. Through their writings, they sought to reveal the true soul of their beloved country. They expressed a love of the countryside and the importance of human will and action. They advocated political liberalism, and in the wake of Spain's loss of her colonies to the United States (1898), staged a literary revival, proclaiming a moral and cultural rebirth for Spain.

The most important of these writers were philosophers Miguel de Unamuno (1864—1936) and José Ortega y Gasset (1883—1955), novelist Pío Baroja y Nessi (1872—1956), and poets Antonio Machado (1875—1939) and Juan Ramón Jiménez (1881—1958), who won the Nobel Prize for his poetry in 1956. Federico García Lorca (1898—1936) was another important literary figure. A supporter of the Republic at the onset of the Civil War, he was murdered by Franco's fascists. As a poet, he was instrumental in bringing new influences into the genre, and his purity of expression brought him fame beyond Spain. Most of his works have been translated into several languages, including English.

Pablo Casals (1876—1973) was lauded as the best cellist of this era. By the age of four years, Casals was playing the piano, at age five he joined the church choir, and by nine he could play the organ and violin. He started

Surrealist painter Salvador Dalí with his signature moustache, holding his famous glass walking stick.

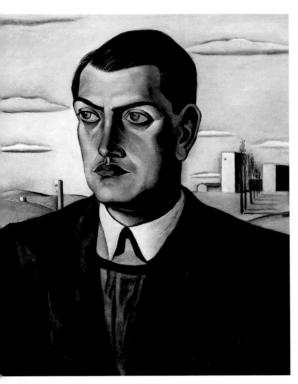

This portrait of Luis Buñuel was painted by Salvador Dalí in 1924.

playing the cello at 11 years of age. In 1890 Casals was in a Barcelona bookstore with his father and found a volume of Bach's six cello suites. The suites were considered musical exercises but Casals saw in them something deeper and when he played them in public his performance shocked listeners by correcting the previously held belief that Bach's solo music for strings had no artistic value or warmth.

Few have been able to match the virtuosity of Andrés Segovia, the late classical guitarist.

21ST-CENTURY ARTISTS

Spain continues to produce artists of extraordinary talent. Testimony to Spain's strong musical tradition, world-renowned operatic tenor Plácido Domingo has a following all over the globe, and especially so in the United States. Since her performance in 1965 in Carnegie Hall in New York, Montserrat Caballé has become one of the world's leading bel canto sopranos. Victoria de los Angeles (1923—2005) made her formal operatic debut in Barcelona in 1945 and continued her concert career into her seventies. Pianist Alicia de Larrocha (1923—2009) is widely acknowledged to have been one of the finest in the world.

Composer and guitarist Paco Peña was born in Cordoba, but in the late 1960s left Spain for London where his recitals of flamenco music captured the public imagination. He has performed as a solo artist in the Royal Albert Hall in London as well as in New York's Carnegie Hall. Francisco Sanchez Gomez was born in Algeciras in 1947. His stage name, Paco de Lucia, is an homage to his mother, Lucia Gomez. The son of flamenco guitarist Antonio Sanchez and the brother of a flamenco guitarist, Ramon, and flamenco singer, Pepe, Paco de Lucia has explored the former accompaniment-only tradition of flamenco guitar to include melodic statements and modern instrumentation. His collaborations have included albums with late flamenco vocalist El Camaron de la Isla and work with American pianist Chick Corea. Spain's contemporary art scene has dealers worldwide scrambling to represent emerging art stars

The most characteristic instrument of Spain is the Spanish guitar. Derived from the Roman cithara, which was brought into Spain around the time of Christ, the Spanish guitar went through many forms before it evolved into the instrument we recognize today. Moorish musicians used a type of guitar that was rounded, resembling a lute. By the 16th century all kinds of guitars were being made and used, some with as few as four or as many as seven strings and with necks of varying sizes. By this time the instrument had come to resemble a very large fiddle and was commonly called vihuela de mano *(vee-hway-lah day mahn-oh), or "fiddle played by hand." The six-string guitar, with a large sound box and long-fretted neck, eventually became the most popular. Andrés Segovia (1893—1987) was acclaimed as the foremost guitarist of his time. He re-established the guitar as a concert instrument in the 20th century, by demonstrating its expressive and technical potential. He continued giving concert performances past the age of 90 years. The guitar suits the Spaniards well, with its integrity, potential for dreamy or impassioned sounds, and rapid rhythms.*

Guillermo Paneque (1963—), Miquel Barcelo (1957—), and Susana Solano (1946—). Filmmakers Pedro Almodóvar (1949—) and Carlos Saura (1932—) have succeeded Buñuel with their talent and worldwide recognition, while writer Camilo José Cela was awarded the Nobel Prize for literature in 1989.

FOLK ART

Traditional crafts have a long history in Spain, and different regions specialize in different items. Ceramics, however, are found just about everywhere in the country.

In every region there is usually one major school devoted to ceramic craftsmanship. Influences range from Moorish to Portuguese to baroque, and techniques are handed down from generation to generation. One main center for ceramics is in Galicia, which is famous for its signature blue and white pieces with bold decorations.

Unglazed pottery of Cartagena and Aracena shows Arabic influence, with the use of decorative motifs. Glazed pottery from Trigueros and La Palma de Condado is basically Portuguese influenced, with predominant shades of blue,

FLAMENCO

The ultimate artistic creation of Spain is undoubtedly the flamenco, an improvised expressive dance originating in Andalusia and renowned worldwide. But performing the flamenco correctly is quite difficult and takes years of instruction and diligent practice.

The flamenco has three elements: song, guitar, and dance. Flamenco dancers combine supple arm and hand movements with complex heelwork. True flamenco dancers never use castanets, a small instrument made of wooden or ivory shells, held in the hand and clapped together to accompany dancing movements, as is often mistakenly thought. Flamenco dance can be joyous, passionate, or very sad.

How the flamenco began in Andalusia remains a mystery, and many theories abound. Probably the most widely accepted is that the flamenco is Indian in origin, brought to Spain by gypsies who later settled in Andalusia. The early gypsies were often referred to as flamencos, meaning either Flemish (possibly because their bright costumes resembled those of Flanders) or flamingo (because as they danced, the men looked like flamingos, brightly colored and balanced on one leg).

The flamenco has many singing styles, but the two main ones are called cante chico *(kahn-tay chee-koh), meaning "small song," and* cante jondo *(kahn-tay hon-doh), which means "deep song." A* cante chico *is lightweight and cheerful, and* cante jondo, *the more important of the two, passionate and sad.* Jaleo *(hah-lay-o) also accompanies flamenco song, an important element of stamping feet, clapping hands, and occasional shouts of "Olé!"*

green, and white. Southern Catalonia is another major area for elaborately decorated ceramics.

Leather craft is widespread in Spain. *Botas* (BO-tuhs), leather wineskins, are popular. Handmade shoes are also popular in Alicante and the Balearic Islands.

Andalusia is famous for its wicker work and basketry of both cane and olive branches. The region's fine embossed leather crafts and filigree silver are creative remnants of the Moors, as are its fine brass and copperware, marquetry (crafts using inlay of wood, ivory, or mother-of-pearl), and woven handicrafts. Andalusia also specializes in exquisite handmade musical instruments, most notably the Spanish guitar.

The Balearic Islands have a long tradition of producing beautiful glasswork, using methods handed down quite possibly from the Moors. The tradition of iron work in Spain is deep-rooted, and there are many schools throughout the country devoted to keeping this particularly Castilian art alive.

The beautiful ceramic-tiled bridge in front of the military academy in Plaza de España, Seville. Each region has its own distinctive type of ceramics that reflects its heritage.

INTERNET LINKS

www.placidodomingo.com/196/intro.php

This is a biography of Placido Domingo, with links detailing his repertoire, performances, and discography.

www.museodelprado.es/en/the-collection/

This website provides information on the collection of works held at the Prado, current exhibitions, educational resources, and the history of the building.

www.cac.es/

This site provides information on the City of Arts and Sciences in Valencia, including what is on, news, events, and activities.

The poet Federico García Lorca once described the flamenco as "the most gigantic creation of the Spanish people."

LEISURE

The crowded Platja de ses Illetes beach on Formentera. Water sports, swimming, and sunbathing are popular activities along Spain's miles of coastline.

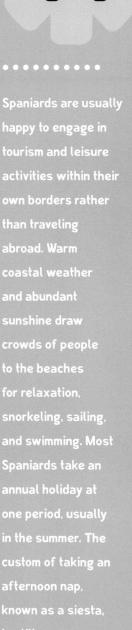

11

S PANIARDS ARE A GREGARIOUS people, filled with energy and the joy of living. This is reflected in the way they enjoy recreational activities. Spaniards spend their leisure time the way most Europeans do—sharing activities with family, socializing with friends, or enjoying sports—and Spaniards do it with gusto.

Their passion can perhaps best be observed at a bullfight, roaring and cheering together as a crowd. The family is the main social unit of Spanish life, and families enjoy spending time together. Weekends are spent with the family as they have little time together during the busy workweek. A typical Saturday or Sunday may include games or a stroll at a nearby park. A religious family goes to church or other places of worship together. The family may also visit relatives, attend a concert, or simply relax at home.

Spaniards are usually happy to engage in tourism and leisure activities within their own borders rather than traveling abroad. Warm coastal weather and abundant sunshine draw crowds of people to the beaches for relaxation, snorkeling, sailing, and swimming. Most Spaniards take an annual holiday at one period, usually in the summer. The custom of taking an afternoon nap, known as a siesta, is still common throughout Spain.

The PortAventura theme park in Catalonia provides entertainment for many families.

A particularly well-to-do family may retreat to a weekend home, perhaps in the countryside, during the more temperate months. Children are adored, and they accompany their parents everywhere. It is not uncommon to see them at bars and restaurants until the wee hours of the morning, waiting patiently as their parents socialize with friends and relatives.

The Spaniard enjoys his or her siesta—that glorious, well-deserved part of the day after lunch, between 1:30 and 4:00 P.M., when most business stops and one takes time to enjoy the quieter side of life. Nearly everyone in Spain observes this ritual, with an afternoon stroll, the traditional nap, or a cup of coffee or glass of wine at a nearby café with friends.

Blessed with a knack for stimulating conversation and the ability to dance, eat, and drink until dawn, the typical Spaniard is a social butterfly. The nightlife is big in Spain, especially in the larger cities, and Spaniards never seem to sleep. They rarely entertain at home, preferring to do so in restaurants or *tapas* (TAH-pahs) bars, where most evenings begin.

After that they go dancing at a local club. The plazas get more crowded as groups of friends gather and talk about anything from politics (Spaniards of all ages are politically versed) to fashion.

SOCCER—THE FAVORITE SPORT

Spaniards love sports, and soccer is their number-one favorite. There are many amateur soccer teams and stadiums all over the country, but the best and most important are located in Madrid and Barcelona. The Spanish league competition began in 1928, but was suspended for three years from 1936 to 1939, the Spanish Civil War period.

The most popular team is Real Madrid, which plays in Madrid's Santiago Bernabéu Stadium, a huge arena with a capacity of 85,454 seats. Real Madrid won the Union of European Football Associations (UEFA) Super Cup in 2002, the UEFA Champion Leagues Cup in 2002, and UEFA Cup titles in 1985 and 1986. The Atlético Madrid team is based just outside the city, and its home base is the Vicente Calderón Stadium. Atlético Madrid won the UEFA Super Cup in 2010. The soccer team of Football Club Barcelona (F. C. Barcelona) won the UEFA Champion Leagues Cup in 2011, the UEFA Cup Winners' Cup in 1997, and the UEFA Super Cup in 2011.

Most Spaniards prefer to watch a soccer match at the stadium, but thanks to television those who cannot be there can still enjoy the game. Soccer players become veritable celebrities in Spain. Many of them earn huge salaries and become millionaires at a young age.

OTHER SPORTS

Sailing and other water sports are also popular with Spaniards. Sailing in particular is a favorite of King Juan Carlos I, who keeps his own fleet of sailboats on Majorca in the Balearic Islands.

Fans of the Spanish national team cheering for their favorite soccer stars.

Golf is another big attraction, and there are excellent courses, especially in the southern regions and along the Mediterranean. Many Spanish golf professionals have gained international fame, most notably Severiano Ballasteros (1957—2011) and Sergio García (1980—).

Tennis is a very popular sport, at social, club, and international levels. The depth of talent in Spanish tennis is enormous. In 2011 there were nine Spanish players in the Association of Tennis Professionals (ATP) top 50 rankings, with three players in the top 10: Rafael Nadal ranked 2; David Ferrer ranked 5; and Nicholas Almagro ranked 10.

Cycling is gaining popularity, especially since Spaniard Pedro Delgado won the Tour de France in 1988. Since then Miguel Indurain has had five consecutive victories, from 1991 to 1995. More recently Oscar Pereiro won in 2006, Alberto Contador won in 2007, 2009, and 2010, and Carlos Sastre won the Tour in 2008. Spain has an equivalent La Vuelta race that started in 1935. Juan José Cobo was the winner of the 2011 La Vuelta. Madrid hosts an annual bicycle day, when cyclists in various states of fitness take to the road.

Snow-skiing is another popular pastime in Spain. With so many mountain ranges, it is possible for Spaniards to ski at most times somewhere in the country. In many cases, a snowy slope is often just a few hours' drive from a sunny beach.

The six major areas for skiing in Spain are the Cantabrian Mountains, the Catalan Pyrenees, the Aragónese Pyrenees, El Sistema Ibérico (the easternmost mountain range), El Sistema Central (close to Madrid in the center of the country), and El Sistema Penibético, the southernmost mountain chain in the heart of the Sierra Nevada.

TRADITIONAL ATTRACTIONS

The Basque national sport is pelota, an extremely fast court game also popular in Latin America and parts of the United States. The Basque name for one variety of pelota is *jai alai* (hi uh-lie), which means "joyous festival." Pelota developed from an ancient rural game that involved hitting a ball against a wall using one's hand.

Pelota—one of the fastest and most strenuous games in the world—is played in a walled concrete court.

Today pelota is more complex and dangerous. Players propel a rock-hard ball against a wall using a long-shaped basket strapped to the wrist. If not using the basket players may protect their hands with materials made of foam-rubber, which may be fixed with bandages or other adhesives. It is forbidden to use any type of protection that will overprotect the hand and increase the power of the stroke. The hand protection may not be more than 10 millimeters (0.39 inches) thick and must be in more than one piece. The type of wall and the size of basket vary according to the difficulty level and type of match. The most common wall is the three-sided *frontón* (fron-TOHN), and the least common, the four-sided *trinquete* (treen-KEH-teh). Walls may be long, short, or slope-roofed. The baskets the players wear may be single-handed or double-handed, rubber- or leather-lined, longer or shorter. The International Federation of Basque Pelota is the official governing body of the sport in Spain. The Federación Internacional de Pelota Vasca (FIPV) considers that there are four different types of court where play takes place (called Modalities), the trinquete and three different-sized fronton courts. Within these Modalities, a Specialty is what is played on that court. There are 14 official Specialties and women may participate in two of them. The finest pelota players in Spain usually do not stay but go to the United States, especially Miami, Florida, to seek stardom there.

BULLFIGHTING

To call bullfighting a sport is not quite accurate. In Spain a bullfight is a spectacle, a ceremony, and a drama.

In fact the Spanish language does not even use the word *fight* in describing the much-loved event. *Corrida de toros* (koh-REE-dah day TOH-ros), which means "running of the bulls," is a more dignified term.

Bullrings are found all over Spain, but the most important are in Madrid and Seville. Indeed there are even museums dedicated to the sport, and many writers and artists have been inspired by the ceremony of the spectacle. American writer Ernest Hemingway immortalized the pageantry and danger of the bullfight in two books, *The Sun Also Rises* and *Death in the Afternoon*.

The origins of bullfighting can be traced back to the Bronze Age in Crete, Greece, when young boys tested their worth by throwing themselves onto the horns of pasturing bulls. During Spain's early Christian age the pastime was outlawed, but it was restored again by the Moors during their occupation.

Since then bullfighting has had a strong following in Spain, if not by the ruling kings and queens, at least by the general population. Interestingly enough, in earlier years, the bullfights were fought by nobles to impress their peers, lady friends, and subjects, and only on horseback.

This changed in the 17th century when paid fighters from the lower classes took over and transformed the event in many ways. A commoner, Francisco Romero, is credited as being the first man in 1725 to have killed a bull on foot, to the delight of the crowd. One of the first bullrings to be built in Spain was in Ronda. It was opened in 1785 with a bullfight featuring Pedro Romero and Pepe Illo. La Venta bullring in Madrid was erected in 1931.

The *corrida de toros* is complex. It always begins with a parade and ceremony. The focal point is the matador, who has assistants on foot called banderilleros, and assistants on horseback called picadores. The assistants enter the ring with the matador and proceed to taunt the animal by waving bright-colored capes and jabbing it with long dart sticks.

The year 1992 was an important one for Spain. The Summer Olympics were held in Barcelona, with a total of 9,356 athletes from 169 countries competing. Spain finished the games with 22 medals overall, 13 of which were gold. The Universal Exhibition of Seville (Expo '92) with the theme of "The Age of Discovery" attracted 41,814,571 visitors. Madrid was designated the Cultural Capital of Europe for 1992. To prepare for the 1992 Summer Olympic Games, Barcelona underwent major renovations. Entire city blocks in unkempt neighborhoods were spruced up or even razed. The main stadiums, which can hold hundreds of thousands of people, were built in the Montjuïc area. And along the sea front, a mini-city was erected to house the 20,000 athletes, trainers, and officials involved in the games. In Madrid a program of restoration was undertaken to transform the Plaza Mayor and its environs. An outdoor sculpture museum, two new theaters, and a new design center were also added to the building program. Like Barcelona and Madrid, Seville also made great efforts to spruce up the city. Roads and airports were improved, new hotels built, and old buildings restored, such as Seville's magnificent Gothic cathedral.

In addition, all over Spain, there were celebrations to mark the 500th anniversary of Columbus's voyage to America and to celebrate the contribution of Jewish and Arab cultures to Spain. After the isolation of the Franco years and the difficult transition to democracy, it was easy to see why the Spaniards were so excited. Spain was participating once again in mainstream European and world culture.

This enrages the bull and gives the matador the chance to observe the bull in action and gauge its temperament. In the finale, the matador, dressed in his bejeweled attire (known as a suit of lights), begins a series of intricate maneuvers with cape and sword, working his way toward the bull. The tension builds until the matador aims for a spot between the bull's shoulders and plunges his sword in. The matador often needs to repeat this until the bull is dead.

Spanish crowds are hard to please. They shout "*Olé!*" and throw flowers into the bullring only if the matador has fought with dignity. A Spaniard knows his bullfight and has high expectations. Afterward a team of horses is led in to help drag the dead bull away. The matador is also presented with ears or the tail of the bull for putting on a good show.

Successful matadors have become wealthy. Some of the more famous ones are Juan Belmonte (1892—1935), Antonio Ordoñez (1932—98), Manuel Benítez, who was known as El Cordobés (1936—), and Manuel Rodríguez Sánchez, also known as Manolete (1917—47), who was killed in the bullring in 1947.

In recent years there have been calls to ban bullfighting, as many consider it to be barbaric and against animal rights. It is also dangerous for the matadors. In 2010 Spanish matador Julio Aparicio needed two operations but was fortunate to escape death after he was horrifically gored through the throat during a bullfight in Madrid.

In 1991 the Canary Islands became the first autonomous community to ban bullfighting. In 2011 the last fight was held in La Monumental in Barcelona after Catalonia also banned the practice.

In Spain, bullfighting is not just a sport but an art that is ancient and traditional, reflecting the psyche of the people.

INTERNET LINKS

www.realmadrid.com/cs/Satellite/en/Prehome_ES2.htm

This is the official website of the Real Madrid soccer team. It includes information on the club, players, matches, ticket sales, stadium, history, and future projects.

www.fun-learning-spanish.com/spanish-tennis-players.html

This website contains many links to interesting facts and figures about Spain, including pages dedicated to Spanish tennis players, fiestas, and artists.

www.fipv.net/en

This is the official website of the International Federation of Basque Pelota, with detailed information on all the complex rules and regulations governing the game.

FESTIVALS

Valencia is famous for an unusual event, Las Fallas of San José. During the week-long feast, huge figures of wood, papier-mâché, and cloth are erected by competing teams in the main plazas.

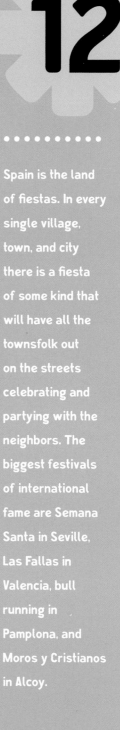

SPANIARDS ENJOY FESTIVALS LIKE few other peoples in the world. They are truly at ease in celebration. In many cases they plan all year for a festival. Spanish celebrations, whose origins may go back hundreds and thousands of years, are steeped in tradition, folklore, history, and regional pride.

There are hundreds of festivals, each an elaborate testimony to Spanish creativity. Fiestas and religious celebrations, both somber and joyous, are observed in accordance with the Christian calendar.

The most important festivals are Holy Week and Corpus Christi. There are *ferias* (FEH-ree-uhs), popular fairs held in towns and villages throughout Spain. Seville's April Fair, for instance, is renowned for its colorful horseback processions and range of activities.

There may be a festival on the occasion of a grape harvest or the selling of livestock. There are festivals that honor an event, person, or moment in history or that herald the beginning of a new season. In addition every town in Spain, no matter how large or small, honors its patron saint with feasting, parades, fireworks, and floats. Music, dance, and bull running are highlights of all fiestas.

Festivals are a time for traditional dress and Old World ways. All the townspeople gather on the streets and in the main square, which are strewn with confetti and flowers. The children especially are a grand sight in their full traditional regalia. Girls have their hair tied back, with a colorful bloom at the nape of their neck. Many of them wear beads and carry flower baskets. Boys wear short, slim-fitting jackets called *boleros* (boh-LAY-rohs), cummerbunds, and hats.

12

Spain is the land of fiestas. In every single village, town, and city there is a fiesta of some kind that will have all the townsfolk out on the streets celebrating and partying with the neighbors. The biggest festivals of international fame are Semana Santa in Seville, Las Fallas in Valencia, bull running in Pamplona, and Moros y Cristianos in Alcoy.

CARNIVAL

Carnival is celebrated all over Spain, symbolizing the final abandonment before Lent, the season of penitence in the Catholic Church. All over the country there is a great display of gaiety, music, decoration, and color, with fancy dress parades, beauty pageants, and dancing in the streets. Cádiz and the island of Tenerife have some of the most spectacular celebrations. Daily activities come to a halt as tourists and Spaniards alike rejoice in the annual festival.

LAS FALLAS

This end-of-winter celebration in Valencia is a week-long fiesta to honor Valencia's patron saint, San José (Saint Joseph), father of Jesus Christ and patron saint of carpenters. According to legend, in the Middle Ages the Brotherhood of Carpenters burned accumulated wood shavings on March 19, Saint Joseph's Day. Today more elaborate activities take place. All usual daily duties cease from March 12 to 19. Huge figures made of cardboard, wood, polyurethane, styrofoam, cork, plaster, and papier-mâché are erected in all the main plazas. These figures, up to 30 feet (9.1 m) high, are often satirical versions of historical and contemporary persons. Every day of the Fallas begins with a wake-up call, La Despertà, at 8:00 A.M. Brass bands march down the streets accompanied by firecrackers. There is feasting, music, dancing, and the first bullfight of the season. At 2:00 P.M. La Mascletà begins—organized pyrotechnical explosions all over the city. Each night there is a fireworks display. Prizes are awarded for the best figure design, fireworks, flower display, and *paella* (pah-AY-ah), a rice-based dish. In a great show of drama, as in the Middle Ages, everything is burned to ashes in collective bonfires the night of the 19th, the Night of Fire.

ROMERÍA

Festivities surrounding a *romería* (roh-meh-REE-uh), or pilgrimage, in Spain mark the journeys of the faithful to specific shrines or sanctuaries. Always

Central to Spanish life are fiestas. During such occasions, the streets are filled with locals dressed for a carnival parade.

accompanied by fanfare of some kind, the festivities begin on the first day of the pilgrimage and end on the saint's day they commemorate.

Undoubtedly the most popular *romería* in Spain is that of Andalusia's El Rocío, marking the end of spring. In the province of Huelva along the Costa de la Luz, in a typical Andalusian procession, people on horseback and in flower-covered wagons and carriages from all over Spain converge to make their way to the shrine of the Virgin of El Rocío in Almonte.

Many days are devoted to prayer, offerings, and celebrating Mass, along with song, dance, and wine-drinking. At dawn on the final day, the statue of the Virgin Mary is removed from its shrine and solemnly paraded through the crowd.

SEMANA SANTA—HOLY WEEK

Semana Santa, or Holy Week, is a week-long celebration commemorating the passion of Jesus Christ. The Spaniards have a gift for ardently reliving the passion. The Holy Week celebration is picturesque, yet it can also be disturbing, as the processions can take on a frightening air.

The activities begin the week before Easter. Massive floats bearing the figures of Christ and the Virgin Mary and depictions of his suffering are carried by costumed penitents chosen from among the people. Before them, and accompanied by drum rolls and the clanking of chains on the pavement, hundreds of robed and hooded penitents walk through the streets to atone for the sins of the past year. The parade of floats is accompanied by beautiful musical compositions, and the penitents chant in time as they bear the floats through the neighboring streets around religious institutions.

Holy Week celebrations in Seville are the most original. Thousands of citizens and tourists line the streets day and night to watch the elaborate floats make their way through the city. All the floats finally converge on Seville's extraordinary Gothic cathedral. The local bars and restaurants are packed every night with participants exhausted from the day's work.

A Holy Week procession in Málaga. One of the most dramatic religious events of the year, Holy Week is celebrated passionately all over Spain.

The San Fermín festival in Pamplona is an exciting spectacle not to be missed.

There are other important Holy Week celebrations as well. In Lorca in the region of Murcia, the townspeople exhibit great imagination as biblical characters are represented by villagers wearing masks.

Valladolid, the capital of Castile-León, is famous for its magnificent though solemn celebration of Holy Week. This features beautiful baroque sculptures and religious figures chosen from their museum, which houses the finest religious icons and statues in the country.

EPIPHANY

January 6, the day of the Epiphany, is also the day of gift-giving in Spain. On this day many towns hold parades for the Three Kings. Floats and figures make their way through streets and plazas, and candies are thrown to children along the route.

On the the night of January 5, the eve of the Epiphany, children put their shoes out on the porch or balcony in anticipation of gifts. They wake up the next morning to find presents inside their shoes, supposedly delivered during the night by the Three Kings.

NEW YEAR'S EVE

New Year's Eve is a family celebration in Spain. Spaniards observe an interesting tradition: at midnight, all members of the family eat one grape for each stroke of the clock and make toasts with glasses of champagne.

SAN FERMÍN—THE RUNNING OF THE BULLS

Every summer, from July 6 to 14, Pamplona celebrates the beginning of its bullfighting season with a week's worth of activities, wine, and gaiety.

Immortalized by Ernest Hemingway in *The Sun Also Rises*, the San Fermín festivities in Pamplona are among the most popular and joyous and possibly the most dangerous for participants.

Very early each morning, the bulls that are to fight in the ring in the afternoon are released into the streets, guided by barriers. Men show their courage and speed by racing ahead of the bulls through the streets to the bullring. Sometimes the participants are wounded or even killed during the run. Nevertheless the many taverns in the area are always filled to capacity every night that week, with brave men proudly recounting their heroic feats.

The running of the bulls in Pamplona also makes for brave little children. Part of the festivities includes the appearance of a man wearing a three-cornered hat, like that of a matador. As children race to get out of his way, the costumed man gives chase and attempts to strike them, to make them behave.

INTERNET LINKS

www.spanish-fiestas.com/spanish-festivals/

This website contains general information on Spanish fiestas as well as a link to a 12-month calendar of Spanish festivals and numerous individual links to particular events around the country.

www.spanish-fiestas.com/spanish-festivals/la-tomatina-tomato-battle-bunyol.htm

This website provides information on La Tomatina, an extremely popular and chaotic event.

www.alcoiturisme.com/moros-y-cristianos/moros-y-cristianos.php?lg=in

This is the official website of Alcoy tourism, with a link to the Moors and Christians Festival, in English. The site also displays lots of images taken during the festival.

The highlight of La Tomatina in Buñol near Valencia is the tomato fight that takes place on the last Wednesday in August and lasts for about an hour around midday. Tens of thousands of tomatoes are brought in by the truckload. One of the rules is that tomatoes must be crushed before they are thrown to avoid injury.

FOOD

This market in La Boqueria, Barcelona, sells all kinds of agricultural produce from Spain's farmlands.

13

THE CUISINE OF SPAIN is as varied as the land. Bordering the Mediterranean Sea, the Atlantic Ocean, France, and Portugal, and having been subjected to many invasions and conquests, Spain has produced a cuisine that is as rich in flavor as it is in history. It is an inspired combination of the very exotic and the very simple.

CULINARY INFLUENCES

The occupation of Spain by the Moors for 750 years greatly influenced Spanish culinary development. Bringing their own rich heritage, the Moorish invaders introduced the cultivation of rice, now a staple food; spices such as saffron, cumin, and anise; nuts; and fruit such as figs, citrus, and bananas.

The Moors also introduced their own methods of food preparation. For instance the technique of marinating fish in a strong, vinegary sauce and the combination of sweet and spicy foods are of Arab origin. From the Spanish conquests in the New World in the 16th century came eggplant, tomatoes, potatoes, red and green peppers both hot and sweet, and chocolate. But Spain is not without its own indigenous culinary features. Just as the Spanish peasants in rural villages ate simple seasonal food for hundreds of years, Spaniards today still eat seasonally, relying on the simple excellence of the natural resources produced by each of the country's regions.

Spain's culinary traditions depend on locally grown vegetables and fruits as well as meats and poultry. *Jamón serrano* (HA-mohn se-RAH-noh), a cured ham, and *chorizo* (choh-REE-soh), a seasoned sausage, are especially favored. Seafood and fish are popular in coastal areas. Other popular foods are cheeses, eggs, beans, rice, nuts (especially almonds), and bread. Olive oil and garlic are common ingredients.

The Mediterranean climate, the lush pastures of the northwest, the Nordic temperatures of the mountain regions, and the seafood-laden coastlines all combine to provide an enormous variety of excellent meat and dairy and agricultural products for Spaniards.

MEALTIMES AND TYPICAL MEALS

Spaniards are known for eating late and not eating light. There is one exception—breakfast. Breakfast, usually served between 7:00 and 8:00 A.M., is simple, often consisting of rolls, butter or preserves, and coffee. This is the only meal where bread is served with butter or preserves, but it is just as likely to be served with olive oil or crushed tomatoes. Spanish coffee is a strong espresso, usually drunk black or mixed with hot milk. For the young at heart, there is also the children's favorite, *churros* (CHOO-ros), strips of sugared fried dough dipped in thick hot chocolate.

Lunch is the main meal of the day for Spaniards. Served between 2:00 and 3:00 P.M., lunch may start with a soup, followed by a salad with a fish or meat course and perhaps some vegetables, or maybe even a hearty paella. Although it is becoming more common in the big cities for working people to grab a sandwich at a nearby tavern or restaurant, the norm is still to eat a big meal in the middle of the day and to eat it leisurely. Lunch is eaten with bread, no butter, and a bottle of wine. Bottles of mineral or tap water are also served at every meal.

Dinner is eaten very late, almost never before 9:00 P.M. and sometimes even as late as midnight. If it is a family meal eaten at home, dinner may be light: a potato omelet served cold, or perhaps cold meat, cheese, and bread. For a social occasion, however, dinner may be different. An evening out with friends is usually preceded by a stop at a tapas bar. The evening begins at around 7:00 P.M.

Tapas, an age-old custom in Spain, can be found all across the country, in big cities as well as in little mountain villages and coastal resorts. It is a special feature of Spanish dining, eaten sometimes before lunch but usually before dinner, and is more a style of eating than a particular food. The types of tapas are as varied as the regions of Spain. They consist of sampling portions of delicacies, first or main courses, or whatever abounds. They can be as simple as marinated olives, grilled sausage, or anchovies on toast. On the other hand, some are as elaborate as an herb-filled rice salad, marinated stuffed squid, or meatballs with saffron sauce. Each bar may have one or more specialties. Cubes of cured ham are also a simple and popular favorite.

As dinner is served so late at night, people still have an appetite after an earlier round of tapas. A typical dinner in a restaurant or bar will consist of a soup, vegetables, and a light meat or fish course. Although Spaniards like to nibble on sweets, cakes, and cookies throughout the day (another legacy inherited from the Moors), they are not really dessert lovers and prefer a piece of fruit or cheese to top off a meal. There is, however, a particular fondness for flan, an egg custard flavored with orange, coffee, chocolate, or caramel. And sweets such as quince paste eaten with fresh goat cheese or a similar cheese are popular.

Locals enjoying some snacks at a tapas eatery in the Mercado de San Miguel in Madrid.

REGIONAL SPECIALTIES

There are many regional foods and as many ways to cook these specialties as there are cooks. To sample all the food that Spain has to offer would be a lengthy and complex culinary journey. From the mountains to the coasts to the plains, there are many dishes, flavors, and aromas.

However, a few similarities unite Spain's regional specialties. Olive oil, for one, is indispensable in preparing many of the dishes.

Spain is basically a rice-eating country, and many dishes are made with rice. They range from the very elaborate to the very simple, as when rice is baked with whatever is handy in the kitchen such as a piece of bacon fat for flavor. One interesting dish is squid ink rice, fried with peas, onions, tomatoes, and garlic.

As in the past, bacalao *is still considered a staple food. Because meat is not eaten during Lent, households rely on a meat substitute that is affordable and that can be stored for days.*

Bacalao needs a lot of preparation, however. Since it must be desalted before cooking, cooks first slap the fish against a hard surface to break down the fibers and then leave it to stand under running water or to soak for at least 24 hours, changing the water frequently. The fish is then simmered gently.

Just as integral to Spanish cooking is the humble egg. Egg dishes are found throughout the country, from restaurants and taverns to the home. The potato omelet, served cold or at room temperature, is a favorite. *Huevos flamencos* (WEH-buhs flah-MEN-kos), fried eggs baked with ham, tomatoes, and vegetables, is traditionally a dish from Seville that is now available all over Spain. Whatever the preparation, Spanish egg dishes are always savory and satisfying.

Also popular are *cocidos* (koh-SEE-dohs), traditional Spanish stews. These are usually a combination of fresh and dried vegetables with different meats. Every region has its own version of this dish, and its own name too: Catalans refer to the dish as *escudella* (eh-scoo-day-yuh), while Andalusians call it *potaje* (poh-tah-hay). Every region also makes great use of chorizo, a spicy smoked sausage. Truly the essence of Spanish cooking, chorizo finds its way into just about every dish.

GREEN SPAIN The northwest is one of the richest areas for food. It is known for its hearty dishes that ward off the chilly weather in the region.

The cuisine of the Basque country is famous for its pork and seafood, such as baby eels cooked in hot oil with hot chilies. Another popular dish is *bacalao* (bah-kuh-LAH-oh), or dried salt cod. One of the most versatile foods in Spain, it can be cooked with onions and peppers or blended into a purée with cream, olive oil, garlic, and other spices. Another interesting way to cook *bacalao* is to slowly simmer it in garlic, which produces a gelatinous sauce with the consistency of mayonnaise.

The Cantabrian valleys produce a variety of pastries, made with the region's excellent dairy produce. High-quality eggs, cheese, milk, and butter are used extensively in Cantabrian cuisine. Two local pastry specialties are *sobaos* (soh-BAH-ohs) and *quesada* (kay-SAH-duh).

Well-known dishes of Asturias are *fabada asturiana* (fah-BAH-duh ass-too-ree-AH-nuh), or butter beans and sausage, and *morcilla* (mor-SEE-yuh), or blood sausage. The region's *picón* (pee-KON) cheese and cider are also popular favorites, served at almost every bar and tavern.

A market store offers meat products from hams to sausages.

The isolated region of Galicia is said to have the finest cuisine in all of Spain, or at least the finest array of fish and shellfish, which the Galicians know how to prepare well. For shellfish, the region boasts oysters, tiny clams, mussels, and shrimp.

From the seas come sardines, hake, cod, and octopus and from the freshwater rivers and streams, trout, salmon, and crayfish. The lamprey eel is another favorite, treasured in Spain since ancient times, and scallops, baked and stuffed, are served everywhere.

Galicia is also famous for the empanada, a small double-crusted pie colored with saffron and stuffed with an array of fillings, from fish to pork to vegetables. It can also be filled with fruit and served as dessert.

Although the origin of the empanada is unknown, it has been popular in Spain for centuries. In the medieval dining hall of Santiago's cathedral monastery, amid the other carvings on display, there is a carved relief of a man holding an empanada.

INLAND SPAIN This is the region of roasts—lamb, veal, suckling pig, kid goat, and other game. Their extraordinary taste and texture come from meticulous roasting in wood-fired clay ovens. Inland Spain also boasts some of the best sausage and cheese products in the world.

La Rioja, a peaceful farming area with an abundance of trout streams, is known as much for its cuisine as for its wine. León's roast suckling pig goes well with the region's strong wines.

La Mancha, also known for its good wines, is the home of Spain's favorite cheese, *manchego* (mahn-CHAY-go). The specialty of Extremadura is its lamb stew, a savory dish boldly seasoned with paprika and recommended only for those with a hearty appetite!

Madrid has no real cuisine of its own, but it does have a number of city-oriented and sweet dishes. The region's *cocido madrileño* (koh-SEE-doh mah-dree-LAY-nyoh) is prepared throughout Spain. It is a stew of chickpeas, vegetables, beef, chicken, bacon, and sausage, served in three courses—the delicious broth as the first course, followed by the vegetables, and then the meats.

THE PYRENEES The cuisine of this region is typically mountain cuisine. Trout and other fish from mountain streams are cooked *a la llosa* (ah lah YOH-sah)—on a slate slab over hot coals. Beef can also be prepared this way. Typical game specialties are stews featuring wild boar or mountain goat. Dishes made with rabbit, quail, partridge, venison, and duck are also popular. In addition wild mushrooms are a local delicacy.

MEDITERRANEAN SPAIN All over the Mediterranean region, virtually every type of seafood makes its way into a meal, from the impressive lobster to baby eels, prawns, spider crabs, and anchovies. Along the Mediterranean, dinner may be a modest yet hearty meal of a simple fish soup, a seafood-stuffed omelet, or a stew of shellfish and fish cooked in a rich tomato sauce.

Catalonia blends the best culinary elements of both France and Spain. Known for garlicky fried croquettes of cod and potatoes, Catalonia is also home to spicy sauces such as *romesco* (roh-MESS-koh), a savory blend of red peppers, hazelnuts, and olive oil, and *alioli* (ah-lee-OH-lee), a garlic mayonnaise used in many local dishes.

Murcia and Valencia are famed for their rice dishes, but perhaps the best loved is native to Valencia. *Paella valenciana* is a flavorful combination of saffron rice, clams, mussels, lobster, fish, chicken, peas, beans, tomatoes, and pimentos.

The amounts vary, but the combinations are important: the red, green, and yellow of the dish are also the colors of Spain. Spaniards eat paella almost exclusively at midday.

SOUTHERN SPAIN The Arab influence on Spain's cuisine is perhaps most apparent in Andalusia, known for spicy sauces, chunky pepper relishes, and herbed marinades. Tapas originated here, and it is said that the best tapas in all of Spain can still be found in Andalusia.

Southern Spain's dishes are simply prepared: grilled onions with herbs, crusty bread, and a sharp red wine. Gazpacho, a cold tomato-based soup with cucumbers, peppers, garlic, oil, and olives, makes a complete meal on its own as it is traditionally served with side dishes like hardboiled eggs, bread, cheese, and wine. Trevelez ham originates from a small village with the same name, and is famous throughout Spain. It is made from white pig and cured in the mountain snow.

A tasty array of Spanish tapas and antipasti.

BALEARIC AND CANARY ISLANDS The cuisine of these islands is exciting and imaginative, as it must sometimes overcome supply shortages. Seafood is at the heart of many of the local dishes but both fish and meat pies are popular everywhere. One example of a traditional dish is a type of flat pizza, brushed with oil and topped with vegetables.

Majorca boasts spicy pork sausages such as *sobrasada* (soh-brah-SAH-duh) and *butifarras* (boo-tee-FAH-ruhs). The former is spiced with red pepper, the latter with cinnamon. *Ensaimada* (ehn-sai-MAH-duh), a traditional sweet bread made of light puff pastry shaped into a coil and dusted with icing sugar, is enjoyed for breakfast, or an afternoon snack, or dessert.

The Canary Islands have many delicious dishes based on the simple combination of fish and *mojo picón* ("moH-hoh pee-Kon"), a spicy and garlicky sauce that gives an unmistakable flavor to island food.

WINE

Wine is consumed at every meal, either straight or diluted with mineral water or soft drinks. Wine has been produced on Spanish soil for thousands of years, beginning with the Phoenician traders in 1100 B.C. and the Romans in 200 B.C.

The wines of Green Spain are slightly acidic and the perfect accompaniment to the seafood dishes of the area.

Galicia's Cambados and Ribeiro wines have gained international attention. The white Ribeiro, traditionally served in little porcelain cups, is quite acidic. The red Ribeiro is robust and popular. Of special interest is the albariño (ahl-bey-REE-noh) wine, a white wine made from grapes introduced by monks traveling on their pilgrimages from the Rhine and Moselle valleys.

The La Rioja region of inland Spain produces the best of Spanish table wines, both prized reds and unique whites. As these wines have grown in fame and popularity, strict regulations have been developed to govern their quality control, production, and labeling so as to prevent fraud.

Catalonia, along the Mediterranean coast, is the home of the exceptional Catalan cava (KAH-vah), a sparkling wine with a taste and quality that competes with French champagne.

Also of note are the fortified wines and smooth brandies of Andalusia in southern Spain. From Jerez de la Frontera come the fortified dry golden wines known abroad as sherries, in honor of the town of Jerez where the first wineries were established.

The Canary Island of El Hierro is home to El Hierro wine, praised by Shakespeare's Falstaff. Wines from the Canaries, particularly the malvasias—anglicized as malmsey—of La Palma and Lanzarote are also prized.

TABLE MANNERS

Spain generally follows continental customs when it comes to table manners. Spaniards eat with the fork in the left hand and the knife in the right. The knife is used to push food onto the fork, and then the fork is raised, upside down, to the mouth. By convention neither fingers nor bread are used to put food onto the fork or into the mouth. Wrists are kept on the table, and diners never rest their hands in their lap.

At a dinner party the guest of honor is seated to the right of the host, while the hostess sits at the other end of the table, opposite the host. There is no pressure on guests who do not partake of a certain food or drink. In fact Spaniards hate to see food wasted and consider it more polite to decline extra helpings than to leave food untouched on the plate. A typical Spanish meal and get-together may last well past midnight.

Manners for eating at tapas bars are quite informal. Olive pits and shells from shrimp are discarded quite naturally onto the floor along with napkins and toothpicks. However, taking up spare seats at a table that's already occupied is considered very rude.

Spaniards are sociable and enthusiastic diners. In restaurants a variety of dishes is usually ordered *para picar* (PAH-rah pee-KAHR)—to nibble on.

INTERNET LINKS

www.spain-recipes.com/index.html

This website contains an extensive selection of regional recipes from all over Spain.

http://mykitcheninspain.blogspot.com/

This is the website and blog of Janet Mendel, an American-born journalist living in Spain with a passion for Spanish food, recipes, and cooking.

www.espavino.com/index_en.php

This website provides detailed information on the wine, wine regions, and wine varieties of Spain.

CHURROS (SPANISH DOUGHNUT)

These fritters are eaten for breakfast, with a cup of hot chocolate or chocolate dip.

2 cups (500 ml) water

2 tablespoons (30 ml) sugar

4 tablespoons (60 ml) olive oil

Pinch of salt

2 cups (500 ml) flour

Canola oil for deep frying

½ cup (125 ml) granulated sugar

1 teaspoon (5 ml) ground cinnamon

In a small saucepan over medium heat, combine water, sugar, olive oil, and salt. Bring to a boil and remove from heat. Stir in flour until mixture forms a ball. Heat canola oil in a deep-fryer or deep skillet to 375°F (190°C). Using a pastry bag, carefully pipe strips of the dough into the hot oil. Fry the strips until golden, and drain on paper towels. Mix granulated sugar and cinnamon. Roll drained churros in granulated sugar and cinnamon.

PAELLA (VALENCIAN RICE IN A PAN)

This hearty dish is popular throughout Spain. This recipe serves six to eight people.

¼ cup (60 ml) olive oil

2 boneless chicken breasts, cubed

½ pound (225 g) pork sausage, cubed

1 pound (450 g) boneless pork, cubed

1 finely chopped large onion

1 green pepper, thin strips

¼ pound (115 g) sliced mushrooms

2 cloves garlic, crushed

Pinch of saffron powder

Pinch of oregano

Salt and pepper to taste

3 cups (750 ml) long grain rice

8 cups (2 L) chicken stock

½ pound (225 g) peeled raw prawns

1½ cups (375 ml) frozen peas

2 medium tomatoes, peeled and cubed

12 clams in the shell

Heat some oil in a pan. Fry chicken, sausage, and pork one after another until lightly golden; set aside. Add more oil to the pan and fry onion, green pepper, and mushrooms. Slowly mix in garlic, saffron, oregano, salt and pepper, and rice; stir for 5 minutes. Add the cooked meat, pour in the stock, and bring to boil. Cover the pan with aluminum foil and bake in preheated oven at 400°F (205°C) for 20 minutes, stirring gently every 5 minutes. Add prawns, peas, and tomatoes, and arrange clams on top. Bake for 10 minutes, until the clams open and almost all the stock is absorbed.

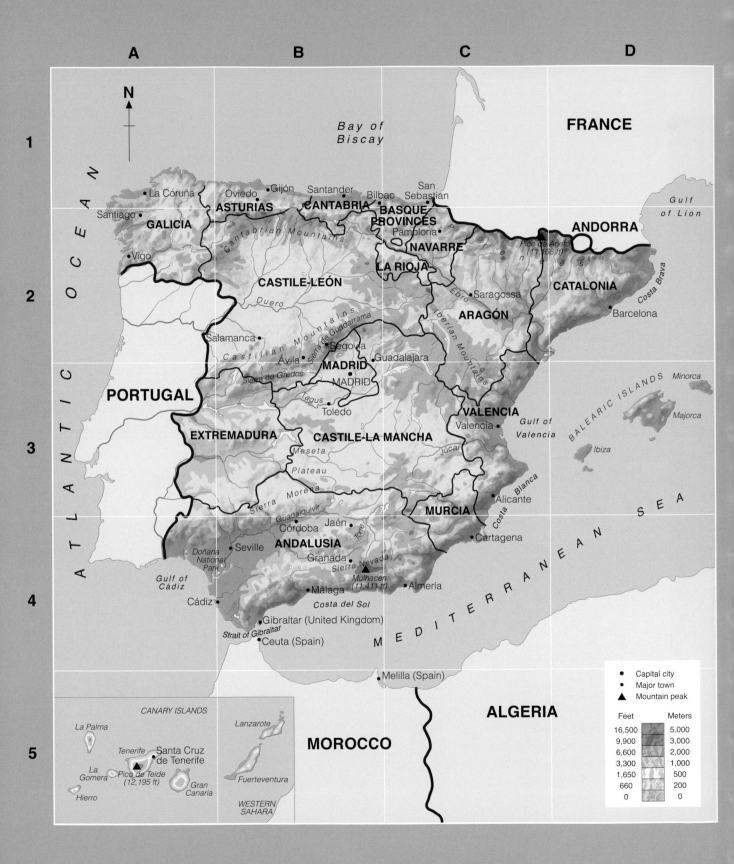

MAP OF SPAIN

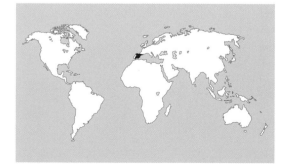

ECONOMIC SPAIN

Manufacturing

- Electronics
- Hydroelectricity
- Iron and Steel
- Shipbuilding
- Textiles
- Toys

Agriculture

- Black bulls
- Cattle
- Citrus fruit
- Olives
- Rice
- Sheep
- Vineyards

Services

- Airport
- Port
- Tourism

Natural Resources

- Fish
- Gold
- Silver

ABOUT THE ECONOMY

OVERVIEW

Spain's economy grew rapidly after it joined the European Community, now called the European Union, in 1986. Unemployment rate fell from 23 percent in 1986 to 8 percent in 2007. Interest rates were reduced and a housing boom further fueled growth. The end of the housing boom in 2007 and the international financial crisis led to a recession in 2008. Housing sales and construction declined and the unemployment rate rose to 26 percent in April 2013. Spain has the highest jobless rate in the 17-nation Eurozone and is expected to slide back into recession, with 5.8 million people out of work.

GROSS DOMESTIC PRODUCT (GDP)

$1.4 trillion
Per capita: $30,400 (2012 estimate)

CURRENCY

The euro (EUR) replaced the Spanish peseta (ESP) in 2002 at a fixed rate of 166.386 pesetas per euro.
1 euro = 100 cents
USD 1 = EUR 0.76 euros (2012 estimate)
Notes: 5, 10, 20, 50, 100, 200, 500 euros
Coins: 1, 2, 5, 10, 20, 50 cents; 1, 2 euros

GDP SECTORS

Agriculture and fisheries 3.3 percent, industry 24.2 percent, services 72.6 percent (2012 estimate)

LABOR FORCE

23.11 million (2012 estimate)

LABOR DISTRIBUTION

Agriculture 4.2 percent, industry 24 percent, services 71.7 percent (2009 estimate)

UNEMPLOYMENT RATE

26 percent (2013 estimate)

INFLATION RATE

2.4 percent (2012 estimate)

MAJOR TRADE PARTNERS

France, Germany, Italy, Portugal, the United Kingdom, the United States

MAJOR EXPORTS

Food products, fruit, minerals, metals, clothing, footwear, textiles, motor vehicles, machinery

MAJOR IMPORTS

Grains, fish, food products, consumer goods, machinery and equipment, fuels, chemicals

MAJOR PORTS AND HARBORS

Barcelona, Bilbao, Cádiz, Cartagena, Ceuta, La Coruña, Málaga, Gijón, Santander, Valencia, Vigo

AIRPORTS

154 total; with paved or unpaved runways (2010 estimate)

CULTURAL SPAIN

Roman Aqueduct
The Roman Aqueduct in Segovia, Castile-León is one of the finest still in operation.

Altamira Caves
The Altamira Caves in Cantabria were discovered in 1869. The paintings date from the Palaeolithic period. Best known are the paintings of bison and other animals on the ceiling of a cave called the Sistine Chapel of quarternary art.

Fiesta of San Fermin
Pamplona, Navarre, is famous for its Fiesta of San Fermin in July. Early in the morning, youths dressed in white with red berets, scarves, and sashes and brandishing rolled up newspapers run through the town together with the bulls. This spectacular event is broadcast live on Spanish television and watched by the entire country.

Theater-Museum
The Theater-Museum in Figueras, Catalonia, created by Salvador Dali, is a world of folly and caprice, a gigantic surrealist object.

Pilgrimage of Santiago
The cathedral built on the site of the first basilica erected over Saint James's tomb shortly after it was discovered is the endpoint of the famous pilgrimage of Santiago, made every year by about 2.5 million people.

Escorial Monastery
The Escorial Monastery near Madrid is a monument to King Philip II. The massive gray granite building has the grandeur of a great palace and the austerity of a dedicated monastery.

Barcelona
Barcelona, Catalonia, offers several cultural treats such as the Museum of Catalonian Art, Antoni Gaudi's Church of the Holy Family, and Guell Park.

The Prado
The Prado in Madrid has an outstanding collection of classical paintings.

Las Fallas
Valencia is known for this fantastic celebration, with a firework display on the last day of the Fiesta of San Jose in March.

Córdoba
In the old quarter in Córdoba, Andalusia, three faiths are represented in architecture: an Islamic mosque; a Christian cathedral, curiously incorporated into the mosque; and a Jewish synagogue.

Roman ruins
The Romans founded Mérida, Extremadura, in 25 B.C. Roman ruins include temples, a theater, and an amphitheater.

Semana Santa
Seville, capital of Andalusia, is famous for the elaborate processions during Semana Santa (Holy Week) followed by the Feria, the April Fair. Its cathedral is the third-largest in Europe, after Saint Peter's in Rome and Saint Paul's in London.

Bullring
The bullring in Ronda, Andalusia, is one of the oldest in Spain. Traditional corridas goyescas, fights in period costumes from the time of Goya, are held annually.

The Alhambra
Muslim architecture in Granada, Andalusia, reached its apex in the Alhambra, one of the most remarkable fortresses ever built, and the Generalife, the summer palace of the kings of Granada.

ABOUT THE CULTURE

OFFICIAL NAME
Kingdom of Spain

NATIONAL FLAG
A broad yellow band across the middle, with thin red strips above and below. The national coat of arms, displayed on the hoist side of the yellow band, consists of the Royal Seal framed by the Pillars of Hercules. The Pillars represent the two promontories (Gibraltar and Ceuta) on either side of the eastern end of the Strait of Gibraltar.

NATIONAL ANTHEM
Marcha Real (Royal March)

CAPITAL
Madrid

MAJOR CITIES
Barcelona, Valencia, Seville, Saragossa, Málaga, Bilbao

POPULATION
47,370,542 (2013 estimate)

LIFE EXPECTANCY
81 years (2011 estimate)

ETHNIC GROUPS
Aragónese, Basque, Catalan, Galician, Roma (gypsy), Valencian

RELIGIONS
Roman Catholic 71 percent, other Christian groups less than 10 percent , Islam, Judaism, Buddhism, Hinduism, and the Bahai faith 10 percent

MAJOR LANGUAGES
Castilian Spanish (official) 74 percent, Catalan 17 percent, Galician 7 percent, Basque 2 percent

ADMINISTRATIVE DIVISIONS
Andalusia, Aragón, Asturias, Balearic Islands, Basque Provinces, Canary Islands, Cantabria, Castile–La Mancha, Castile-Leon, Catalonia, Extremadura, Galicia, La Rioja, Madrid, Murcia, Navarre, Valencia

NATIONAL HOLIDAYS
New Year's Day (January 1); Epiphany, (January 6); Saint Joseph's Day (March 19); Victory Day (April 1); Holy Week (March/April); Feast of San Fermin (July 6—14); Saint James's Day (July 25); Assumption Day (August 15); Hispanic Day (October 12); All Saints' Day (November 1); Immaculate Conception (December 8); Christmas Day (December 25)

LITERACY RATE
97.7 percent (2010 estimate)

TIMELINE

IN SPAIN	IN THE WORLD

13,000 B.C.
Stone Age inhabitants paint images of animals on the walls of caves at Altamira.

1100 B.C.
Phoenicians colonize Cádiz and Almuñécar.

550 B.C.
Greeks settle on the East Coast.

237–218 B.C.
Carthaginians conquer southern Spain.

218–201 B.C.
Romans conquer much of Spain.

A.D. 507
Visigoths establish a kingdom in the north; Vandals settle in Andalusia.

A.D. 711
Muslims from North Africa sweep into Spain and destroy the Christian Visigothic kingdom.

A.D. 912–961
Reign of Caliph Abd-al-Rahman III marks the height of economic and cultural splendor in Muslim Spain.

1206–1368
Genghis Khan unifies the Mongols and starts conquest of the world. At its height, the Mongol Empire under Kublai Khan stretches from China to Persia and parts of Europe and Russia.

1479
Ferdinand and Isabella, the Catholic kings, begin joint rule.

1480
Establishment of the Spanish Inquisition

1492
Granada, the last Moorish stronghold, falls. Christopher Columbus sails to the Americas.

1516
Charles I inaugurates Hapsburg rule.

1700
Hapsburg rule in Spain ends.

1789–99
The French Revolution

1808
Napoleon forces Charles IV to abdicate in favor of Napoleon's brother, Joseph Bonaparte.

1873
First Spanish Republic is declared.

1914
World War I begins.

1936–39
Spanish Civil War; General Francisco Franco becomes military dictator.

1939
World War II begins.

1947
Spain is declared a monarchy with a king to be named to succeed Franco.

1955
Spain joins the United Nations.

IN SPAIN	IN THE WORLD
1975 Franco dies; Juan Carlos I ascends the throne.	
1982 Spain joins NATO.	
1986 Spain joins the European Community.	
1992 Summer Olympics in Barcelona	
1996 José María Aznar López becomes president.	
	1997 Hong Kong is returned to China.
2002 The euro replaces the peseta; Ecological disaster on the northwest coastline after oil tanker *Prestige* sinks and breaks up off the coast.	
2003 62 Spanish peacekeepers die in a plane crash while returning from Afghanistan.	**2003** War in Iraq begins.
2004 Jose Luis Rodriguez Zapatero wins the general elections and becomes prime minister.	**2004** Eleven Asian countries are hit by giant tsunami, killing at least 225,000 people.
2005 In defiance of the Roman Catholic Church, parliament legalizes gay marriage and grants homosexual couples the same adoption and inheritance rights as heterosexual couples.	**2005** Hurricane Katrina devastates the Gulf Coast of the United States.
2006 Parliament denounces Franco's rule and orders the removal of all Franco statues, symbols, and street signs.	
2008 Unemployment rate reaches 11.3 percent, with 2.6 million people out of work.	**2008** Earthquake in Sichuan, China, kills 67,000 people.
2009 Spanish economy enters recession. Unemployment rate rises to 19.4 percent.	**2009** Outbreak of flu virus H1N1 around the world
2010 Unemployment rate climbs to over 20 percent. Parliament approves austerity package.	
2011 New conservative government headed by Prime Minister Mariano Rajoy takes up office.	**2011** Twin earthquake and tsunami disasters strike northeast Japan, leaving more than 14,000 dead and thousands more missing.
2013 Unemployment rate reaches 26 percent, with more than 5.8 million people out of work.	

GLOSSARY

bachillerarato (bah-CHEE-yay-re-RAH-toh)
A countrywide examination that students take at the end of their secondary education.

banderillero
A man on foot who assists the matador.

bolero (boh-LAY-roh)
A waist-length, slim-fitting jacket for boys, worn open in front.

conversos (con-BER-sos)
Jews who were forced to convert to Catholicism by the Spanish Inquisition.

corrida de toros (koh-REE-dah day TOH-ros)
"Running of the bulls," or a bullfight.

Euskera (yoo-SKAY-rah)
The Basque name for the Basque language.

feria
A fair, generally held on festive occasions.

flamenco
A world-renowned dance style originating from the Andalusian gypsies, marked by stamping of feet and clapping.

gitanos (hee-TAH-nos)
A group of gypsies living in southern and central Spain.

gusto (GOO-sto)
Great pleasure.

huerta (wehr-tah)
A private garden.

Marranos (mah-RAH-nos)
False Jewish converts to Catholicism who secretly practiced their Jewish faith during the Spanish Inquisition.

Moriscos
Moors who converted to Catholicism during the Spanish Inquisition.

ojalá (o-ha-LAH)
A common expression meaning "I hope it may come to pass."

picador (pee-kuh-dor)
A man on horseback who assists the matador.

romería (roh-meh-REE-uh)
A pilgrimage.

si Dios quiere (see dee-AWS kee-AY-reh)
A popular expression meaning "if God wants to" or "God willing."

tapas
A snack served in many Spanish bars, typically with a glass of beer or wine.

toros bravos (TOH-rohs BRAH-bos)
Bulls bred to fight in a ring.

zarzuela (zar-zoo-EH-lah)
Traditional Spanish operetta.

FOR FURTHER INFORMATION

BOOKS

Inman, Nick, Mary-Ann Gallagher & Josephine Quintero. *Spain* (Eyewitness Travel Guides). New York: DK Publishing, 2011.

Payne, Stanley G. *Spain: A Unique History.* Madison, WI: University of Wisconsin Press, 2011.

Phillips, William D. & Carla Rahn Phillips. *A Concise History of Spain.* Cambridge, England: Cambridge University Press, 2010.

Roden, Claudia. *The Food of Spain.* New York: Ecco, 2011.

Steves, Rick. *Spain.* Berkeley, California: Avalon Travel Publishing, 2012.

Tremlett, Giles. Ghosts of Spain: Travels Through Spain and Its Silent Past. New York, Walker & Company, 2008.

Williams, Mark R. *The Story of Spain: The Dramatic History of Europe's Most Fascinating Country.* Rancho Mirage, CA: Golden Era Books, 2009.

WEBSITES

CIA The World Factbook: Spain. www.cia.gov/library/publications/the-world-factbook/geos/sp.html

Guardian News: Spain. www.guardian.co.uk/world/spain

Spain.info. www.spain.info/en

FILMS

Agora. Focus Features, Newmarket Films, Telecinco Cinema, 2009.

El Cid: The Legend. Filmax Animation, 2003.

Flamenco from A to Z. Long Branch, New Jersey: Kultur, 2010.

Three Steps Above Heaven. Warner Bros, 2010.

MUSIC

De Lucia, Paco. *El Flamenco Es. Paco de Lucia.* Barcelona, Spain: Universal Music, 2010.

Figueras, Montserrat & Jordi Savall. *Cancons de la Catalunya millenaria.* Barcelona, Spain: Alia Vox, 2011.

Iglesis, Julio. *Julio Iglesias "1".* Spain: Jungle Aire / Sony BMG, 2011.

Anillo, Encarna. *Barcas de plata.* Spain: Flamenco World Music, 2008.

BIBLIOGRAPHY

BOOKS

Aviva, Elyn. *Following The Milky Way: A Pilgrimage on the Camino de Santiago.* Boulder, Colorado: Pilgrim's Progress Inc., 2003.

Batali, Mario. *Spain . . . A Culinary Road Trip.* New York: ECCO, 2008.

Crow, John A. *Spain: The Root and the Flower: An Interpretation of Spain and the Spanish People.* Berkeley, CA: University of California Press, 2005.

Haas, Ken. *Flamenco.* London, England: Thames & Hudson, 2000.

Hodges, Gabrielle Ashford. *Franco: A Concise Biography.* New York: Thomas Dunne Books, 2002.

Kurlansky, Mark. *The Basque History of the World.* New York: Penguin USA, 2001.

Lior, Noa. *Spain: The Culture.* New York: Crabtree, 2001.

Van Hensbergen, Gijs. *Gaudi: A Biography.* New York: Harper Collins, 2001.

Vincent, Mary. *Spain, 1833-2002: People and State.* New York: Oxford University Press, 2008.

Williams, Mark R. *The Story of Spain. The Dramatic History of Europe's Most Fascinating Country.* Golden Era Books, 2009.

WEBSITES

Central Intelligence Agency World Factbook (select "Spain" from the country list). www.cia.gov/cia/publications/factbook

Embassy of the United States in Madrid. http://spanish.madrid.usembassy.gov/

Flamenco-world.com (comprehensive information). www.flamenco-world.com/flamenco.htm

International Education in Spain. www.spainexchange.com

Learn Spanish (with audio tutorials). www.studyspanish.com

Lonely Planet World Guide: Destination Spain. www.lonelyplanet.com/spain

Official site of the King of Spain. www.casareal.es/

Official site of the President of Spain (with English version). www.lamoncloa.gob.es/home.htm

Official site of the Senate of Spain. www.senado.es/home_i.html

"Sí, Spain" (news on Spanish current affairs and cultural developments). www.sispain.org

The World Bank Group (type "Spain" in the search box). www.worldbank.org

INDEX

INDEX